BREAKIN
The story of Wil

BREAKING GROUND
The story of William Thomas Mulvany

JOHN J. O'SULLIVAN

MERCIER PRESS
Douglas Village, Cork
www.mercierpress.ie

Trade enquiries to COLUMBA MERCIER DISTRIBUTION,
55a Spruce Avenue, Stillorgan Industrial Park, Blackrock, Dublin

© John J. O'Sullivan

ISBN: 1 85635 427 X

10 9 8 7 6 5 4 3 2 1

This book is sold subject to the condition that it shall not, by way of trade or otherwise, be lent, resold, hired out or otherwise circulated without the publisher's prior consent in any form of binding or cover other than that in which it is published and without a similar condition being imposed on the subsequent purchaser.

Printed in Ireland by ColourBooks Ltd

Contents

Acknowledgments   9

Foreword   11

1 *Ireland in the Early Nineteenth Century*   13
   Economic and Social Status of the Population

2 *The Mulvanys in Dublin*   17
   Painters, Engineers, Architects – William Thomas, Land Surveyor

3 *William Thomas Joins the Board of Public Works*   22
   Drainage of Shannon Basin – Shannon Navigation Laws of 1839 – Feasibility Study and Plans for Shannon–Erne Waterway

4 *Appointed Assistant Commissioner in 1842*   28
   Responsibility for All-Ireland Arterial Drainage, later Inland and Coastal Fisheries – Brother Thomas John joins Board of Works

5 *The Plight of Tenants and Rural Workers*   33
   Population 8.5 million – 27% Paupers – Emigration – The Great Famine – Mulvany's Management of Same – Relief Works

6 *1847 – Effects of Famine*   37
   Board of Works pleads with Westminster for additional finance – 121 Major drainage projects in operation

7 *Aftermath of the Famine*   40
   Some landlords' objections to Board of Works Decisions – Summary Proceedings Act – Lord Rosse and the enquiry by select committee of House of Lords

8 *Mulvany Resigns on Pension*   49
   Meeting with Michael Corr van der Maeren – their visit to the Rhineland – First Impressions

9 *Raising Venture Capital in Ireland*   54
   Securing technology in Durham and Northumberland – Recruitment of English miners – The Irish Investors – Mulvany in sole charge of project

10 *Mulvany Family Moves to Düsseldorf*   60
   Close liaison with Dortmund Mining Office – commencement of work on Hibernia

11 *Modern Technical Systems and Equipment*	66
The 'Tübbing' Development – output of coal 18,000 tons per annum in 1858 – 852 workers employed – Shamrock Mine opened in Herne	
12 *Technical and Commercial Management*	72
Conditions in the mines – competition from UK coal exporters – disagreement among Irish shareholders	
13 *Mulvany Made First Freeman of Gelsenkirchen*	76
Sale of Hibernia and Shamrock to Berliner Handelsgesellschaft	
14 *The Prussian Mining and Iron Company*	79
Mulvany's engagement in trade and commerce – establishment of the Dortmund Mining Association – Delegation's Visit to UK Collieries – first memorandum on Iron and Coal Industry	
15 *Mulvany's Interest in International Communications*	82
16 *Europe's Railways*	85
17 *Mulvany and the Infrastructure*	88
Founder and president of the Long Name Association	
18 *A Man of Means and Influence*	93
19 *Düsseldorf's Harbour and Main Railway Station*	103
The canals – co-founder of Stock Exchange	
20 *Mulvany's Hour of Glory*	108
Public recognition – his death in Düsseldorf-Pempelfort	
Appendix I	120
Transcript of 'A Few Friendly Words to Employers and Employees' by W. T. Mulvany, Düsseldorf 21 June 1872	
Appendix II	130
Translation of Letter of Address to the chaplain of the Irish workers in Gelsenkirchen	
Appendix III	132
The Irish Sea Cross-Channel Sailings 1860–1872	
Appendix IV	133
Share Transfers	
Appendix V	134
List of Memoranda by William Thomas Mulvany during his residence in Düsseldorf 1856–1885	

Appendix VI 136
    Transcript of 'International Communication in the North and East of Europe through the New Harbour of Flushing at the Mouth of the Scheldt in Holland' by W. T. Mulvany

Appendix VII 151
    Notes on the Principal Investors – the Malcolmson Brothers and Henry Bewley

Appendix VIII 154
    Mulvany Family Tree (in part)

Bibliography 156

Index 158

DEDICATED TO
ANNEGRET, ANNE-NUALA AND DONAL
GLÜCK AUF!*

*Miners' greeting/blessing

Acknowledgments

I wish to acknowledge with thanks the generous assistance received in my research from: The Stadtarchiv, Düsseldorf; the Stadtarchiv, Gelsenkirchen; the Stadtarchiv, Herne; the Stadtarchiv Castrop-Rauxel; the Rheinisch-Westfälische Wirtschaftsarchiv, Köln; the Bergbau-Bücherei, Essen and its successor, the Bergbaubibliothek des Ruhrgebiets, Bochum; the Deutsche Steinkohle AG, Herne; Stadtarchiv Datteln; the Bergbau-Museum, Bochum; the Office of Public Works, Dublin; the Department of Agriculture and the late A. O'Loan, Dublin; the Public Records Office, London; the Trustees of the National Library, Dublin; the Institution of Engineers of Ireland, Dublin; the proprietors Haus Goldschmieding, Castrop-Rauxel; Lord Rosse, Birr Castle, Birr; Prof. Thomas Seebohm, Bonn; Mrs N. Prestidge, New Zealand; Mrs Teresa Elliott, New Zealand; Dame Beulah Bewley, DBE, London; Mrs Mary Bewley, Leixlip; Mr Donal Moore, City Archivist, Waterford; Mr J. Cahill, Birr UDC; Waterways Ireland, Carrick-on-Shannon; Rev. Dr Ross Buchman, Christ Church, Düsseldorf; Irish Times Ltd., Dublin.

For the photographs and illustrations used: Bergbau-Bücherei, Essen; Mrs Mary Bewley, Leixlip, Co. Kildare; Rev. Ross Buchman, Christ Church, Düsseldorf; Mr Jackie Cahill, Birr; Mrs Nancy Prestige, Kati-Kati, NZ; Rheinisch-Westfälisches Wirtschaftsarchiv; Royal Dublin Society; Stadtarchiv Castrop-Rauxel; Stadtarchiv Datteln; Stadtarchiv Düsseldorf; Stadtarchiv Herne; Treasury Minutes; Stephan Wieland.

Note: Most of Mulvany's papers, letters, and other records were archived upon the death in 1917 of his daughter, Annabella, in the Rheinisch-Westfälische Wirtschaftsarchiv in Cologne. Most were destroyed, probably in the 1,000-bomber raid on the city in the spring of 1942. However, and fortunately for the record, some items which originally had been misfiled, were discovered in recent years by the present director, Dr Ulrich Soénius, to whom I am indebted for placing these at my disposal. They include photographs of the original Irish investors.

Foreword

When first I came to the Rhineland in 1962 for the IDA (Irish Industrial Development Authority) with the remit to encourage German and other European industrialists to make direct investments in Ireland, I was fascinated by a story I was told about another Irishman who, a century earlier, had encouraged his friends in Ireland to invest in the then under-developed German coal-mines. These Irish investors, perhaps unwittingly, played a significant part in the development of the Rhineland and Westphalia as one of Europe's major industrial regions.

The name of William Thomas Mulvany, from Sandymount, Dublin, is recorded with honour and respect for his achievements in several cities in what has since become the Ruhrgebiet. Mulvany was one of its founding fathers. His contribution to various aspects of the national economy, in coal-mining, town-planning, infrastructure, communications as well as monetary and fiscal policy and commercial institutions, was significant.

Mulvany, the innovator, was an avid writer of memoranda and commentaries on the issues of his day. Unfortunately, most of his private correspondence, which had been archived, was destroyed during air attacks on Cologne in the Second World War. In the early 1900s his daughter Annabella, who died in 1917 in Düsseldorf, tried to have a biography published and after some efforts by writers the journalist Kurt Bloemers, with the support of the Westfälische Wirtschaftsarchiv, published a biography in 1922. Were it not for this record, which I gratefully acknowledge as a major source, for he had access to the family papers, we would know little today about this remarkable man from Sandymount. In gathering together the various strands of Mulvany's career (or, rather, two careers), which have survived, I have endeavoured to place on record these achievements for the benefit of those who may be interested in the unique role of these Irish merchant princes in the mid-nineteenth century on the continent of Europe.

Mulvany's foresight and courage at a time when Ireland was on her knees after the Famine and Prussia had not yet savoured the fruits of the industrial revolution, was unique. It led, *inter alia*, to the formation many years later of Germany's fourth largest industrial conglomerate, VEBA, with a DM 60 billion turnover in chemicals, energy, oil, transport and telecommunications. In June 2000, VEBA merged with the Munich-based VIAG conglomerate under the name E-on. The slender plants of Hibernia, Shamrock and Erin, put down by Mulvany in 1856 in Gelsenkirchen, Herne and Castrop-Rauxel have borne fruit well into the twentieth and twenty-first centuries.

Alas, Mulvany was not a prophet in his own land and there is, up to now, no public recognition of him and his work during the Famine in Ireland. Perhaps this record will help to redress such an unhappy omission.

1

Ireland in the Early Nineteenth Century

In the early years of the nineteenth century, Ireland was beginning to shake off some vestiges of domination and exploitation to which Britain had subjected her in previous centuries. Despite the failure of the 1798 Rising, there was a burgeoning, more articulated, more organised move for independence throughout the country, and many from within the ascendancy class began to see Ireland as a separate nation, politically and culturally.

The Pale of Dublin represented British rule and the extended arm of Westminster was the viceroy in Dublin Castle, aided by a loyal civil service, police and army. In 1829, Daniel O'Connell, lawyer and Member of Parliament, won Catholic Emancipation, perhaps the most important first step forward towards a free, independent island of Ireland.

The bulk of the population were farmers or farm labourers who languished under an inequitable legal and social system. Large tracts of the best land were vested in landlords loyal to the crown, some with hereditary seats in the House of Lords. Many were rare visitors to their Irish properties, leaving the control of the lands in the hands of stewards and agents. If their tenant farmers were unable to pay rent, they were evicted from their holdings and their cottages torn down. A not too enlightened government established workhouses for the poor which were intended to create a basic form of employment but were administered in such a way that they were considered by the inmates to be worse than jails.

A German traveller in Ireland at that time wrote:

> I used to pity the poor Latvians in Livonia. Well, Heaven pardon my ignorance. Now I have seen Ireland, it seems to me that poverty among the Latvians, the Estonians, and the Finlanders is such that they lead a life of comparative comfort.

The Duke of Wellington, born in Ireland, said: 'There never was a country in which poverty existed to the extent it exists in Ireland'.

Strong class divisions marked rural and urban communities, as, indeed, was also the case in England, Scotland and Wales, and remained so well into, and beyond, the industrial revolution. Disraeli commented: 'Britain has two nations, the rich and the poor'. And there were several layers of society within each of these divisions.

In Ireland, as in England, land was the basis of power and influence. The poor Shropshire lad Robert Clive (1725–1774), who later won most of India for the British empire, was not well received upon his return to London, primarily because he had no estate there. He overcame this obstacle by purchasing land in Ireland, then became a Member of Parliament and was created Baron Clive of Plassey in the Irish Peerage.

The root of the problem in Ireland was on the land. Extremely bad relations existed between landowners, mostly descended from settler families from England and Scotland, and their tenants. The conacre system bordered on slavery. Many landlords, though not all, were primarily interested in extracting as much money as possible from their tenants. Under this system, landless people rented the ground to plant and grow crops. Usually there was no legal lease offered and the tenant would not have the ten pounds sterling to pay the stamp duty. So the tenant farmer had no security. If the weather was favourable and the crop was good, he and his family would have food for the following season and he could pay the rent. On the other hand, if the weather was bad and the crop failed which it often did, he and his typically large family could be destitute. There was little incentive for both parties to invest in improving the land. Life on the land was a desperate game of chance.

In 1841, 45% of all holdings were less than 5 acres (2.5 hectares) but an acre and a half could provide potatoes for a whole year for a family of 5 or 6 persons. According to a survey, nearly half of the population were living in window-less mud cabins of a single room. West of the Shannon and in Kerry and Cork this proportion was two-fifths of the population. Over 70% of the population was considered illiterate. Statistics took little account of the rich oral and cultural traditions of the Irish language and culture dating back over very many centuries.

At the end of the eighteenth century there was a Protestant monopoly of officially supported education in Ireland, at a time when the division was roughly 75% Catholic and 25% Protestant. The Catholic clergy were trying to establish their own schools. Conversion from one faith to the other was not uncommon. Well-meaning Protestant relief organisations offered not only food to the impoverished but also sustenance within their flock.

The first seminary for Catholic priests, who earlier had to travel to Salamanca, Louvain and Rome to be educated, was opened in

1790 in Carlow. Seminaries in Kilkenny, Killarney and Belfast followed. Maynooth College was founded in 1814. The Jesuits, who had been mainly concerned with the poor of Dublin from 1750 onwards, opened their prestigious Clongowes Wood College for the children of better-off Catholic families. To cater for the poorer sections of society the Christian Brothers opened their first national and secondary schools in Waterford in 1802. This order opened schools all over Ireland and later in the United States and in India.

In 1831, the Chief Secretary for Ireland, E. G. Stanley, proposed a National Board of Education to support the establishment of inter-denominational schools. This met with universal approval initially but later became controversial. The aim was to provide a better classical education but, as the teaching of the Bible was not allowed, it was opposed by clergy from both the Catholic and Presbyterian communities. Later, the national school system and the model system on denominational lines proved their value in educating the masses, albeit perpetuating the divisions within the population.

Some observers from abroad were able to cast a critical eye on the conditions in Ireland in this part of the nineteenth century. One such traveller, Graf Pückler (Hermann von Pückler-Muskau), a friend of Goethe, who had spent months in the country in 1828, said:

> This kingdom has more in common with Germany than with England. Almost every over-refined industry and culture vanishes here, unfortunately also the English cleanliness. Houses and streets look dirty, though Dublin is endowed with many impressive palaces and wide, aligned streets. The people look shabby, the educated people one meets are without the English elegance, although the number of shining uniforms, which one does not see in London's streets, makes one feel that one is on the Continent ... the great sweep of the landscape, the bay, the far hills of Wicklow, the amphitheatre-like mass of the buildings, the quays, the harbour, are beautiful.

Pückler was a welcome guest in many of the big houses. As he discovered, the island was blessed with a mild, agreeable climate, the mountains all round the coast sheltered rich, arable land, though half of this land was used only for grazing cattle, sheep and horses. Industries, mainly small family-owned enterprises, were concentrated in the larger towns. These included breweries, distilleries, bacon-curing, butter-making, milling, but very little engineering. The major part of the industrial economy was concentrated in the northern province of Ulster where the linen and cotton industries, ship-building as well as their ancillary industries, were located.

This concentration of manufacturing industry was a direct result of the earlier Plantation of Ulster when the government of the day decided to move large numbers of Irish Catholic farmers out of their holdings in Ulster and give them to Protestant families brought over from Scotland and Wales. This form of 'ethnic cleansing' was repeated in Queen Anne's reign when Protestant families from the Pfalz province of Germany, who were refugees from Louis XIV in France, were brought over and settled with plots of land in counties Limerick and Tipperary. Once again, the aim was to strengthen the numbers of Protestants in the country, but the Palatines, who brought good farming skills with them, never integrated into the local communities, largely due to the barriers of language and customs. It took a long time for them to be assimilated among the native Irish. The names of Shoemacker, Bethel, Switzer, Schultheiss (Shouldice), etc., are still to be found in these counties.

A number of rivers, including the 350 km long Shannon, served as natural drainage basins for the rich farmland in the interior of the country. Several of these rivers were navigable. Sailing vessels and steamers could reach the hinterland of Limerick 90 km from the west coast. Here the pastures of the Golden Vale produced beef, milk and butter as well as fine horses. Oats and wheat crops were ground and dried in numerous water-driven mills scattered around the country.

Land agitation during the previous century had left its scars on the rural population and continued to do so right up to the dawn of the twentieth century. Under the leadership of Henry Grattan, a degree of relief from the rigid control of Westminster was won. The Catholic Relief Bill of 1793 had given Catholics the right to vote, and, almost as important, it abolished the barriers which had prevented their being employed in the civil administration.

Larger scale industrial operations as well as the main organs of the country's administration were concentrated in Dublin. A logical consequence of this was that wealth and power resided mainly in the capital and its environs.

2

The Mulvanys in Dublin

In the early 1800s, Sandymount was, and still is, a fashionable residential suburb about six kilometres from the city centre and lies close to the seashore with its distinctive Martello Towers, constructed in the late eighteenth century to deter Napoleon from attacking.

Thomas James Mulvany was one of the co-founders, professor and keeper of the Royal Hibernian Academy in Dublin. He lived in Sandymount, though the address is not known. He was a painter of some repute as was his brother, John George. Later the family moved to Dirker Lodge, Cross Avenue, Booterstown, Co. Dublin (since demolished). A number of paintings by the Mulvany brothers are on permanent exhibition in the National Gallery while others are believed to be in private ownership. The Mulvanys painted landscapes and were commissioned to paint many portraits of prominent personalities, including John Banin, the writer, Tom Moore, the composer, and Daniel O'Connell, lawyer and Member of Parliament, who became known as the Liberator for his achievement in winning Catholic Emancipation for Ireland.

Some records, including a reference by Annabella Mulvany, seem to suggest that the Catholic Archbishop G. Magee of Dublin raised Thomas John and George Mulvany. But there was no Catholic archbishop of that name, there was, however, an Anglican Archbishop Magee (1766–1831). When William Thomas became engaged to Alicia Winslow, a Catholic, his father, Thomas James, wrote to his son expressing concern about problems that might arise from a mixed marriage. This would seem to indicate that he was Anglican. Thomas James died in 1845. He and his wife Mary (née Field) had seven children, William (1806), Eliza, George (1809), Richard John, (1813), Mary, and Thomas John (1821). Births and deaths were not officially registered in Ireland until about 1845, hence the missing dates. Of the fourth child, Richard John, very little is known – one source suggests that he became a publisher of magazines in Dublin.

George (Field) Mulvany followed in the footsteps of his father and uncle and became a painter and later director of the National Gallery of Ireland on its foundation. The livelihood of a painter, however talented, and particularly one with a large family, was none too secure in Dublin at that time. There was a dependence upon the better-off classes for commissions. Yet, the Mulvany home in Sandymount became a rendezvous for writers, artists and musicians as well as members of the establishment with an interest in painting. John (Skipton) Mulvany, W. T.'s brother, became an architect. He designed the Great Southern Hotel in Galway and Broadstone Railway Station in Dublin. He also had some responsibility for the design of Ringsend Dock in Dublin. He was close to the Perry family who were brewers and shareholders in the new railways. He designed a number of station houses, including that at Athlone. He also designed some memorials in Mount Jerome Cemetery in Dublin. In Kingstown (Dun Laoghaire) he designed the Salthill Hotel as well as an extension to the Royal St George Yacht Club and later the Royal Irish Yacht Club. In 1850, he designed Mount Anvil House.

William Thomas, the eldest son, was born on 11 March 1806, and died at the age of 79. Throughout his long life, he appears to have remained in close touch with his roots and family. Indeed, in later years, there is some evidence of nepotism in the furtherance of careers, but this was not considered negative, especially where large families were concerned.

Notwithstanding some accounts that his father and uncle were raised as Catholics, William Thomas was sent to Dr Wall's School in Hume Street, a Protestant institution. At 16, William Thomas converted to the Protestant faith. It is presumed that this was through the encouragement of the school's headmaster and William was probably planning his future and hoping for a university education – this would be easier for him as a member of the Protestant community. Trinity university was the Mecca for many bright and ambitious young people at that time. Although from 1793 Catholics were allowed to enter Trinity as students they had to get permission from their bishop, and this was not always easy. They were excluded by the university from holding fellowships.

The young Mulvany did secure a place at Trinity and enrolled in the medical faculty – looking forward to a life as a doctor. However, his hopes were dashed at a very early stage: he had been in Trinity only a few months and his father could not afford the fees due to financial difficulties. William Thomas was forced to abandon his aspirations for a third level education and leave the college. It was the first of two major crossroads at which William Thomas found himself during his life.

Fortunately, this setback coincided with a major government

project being undertaken, namely the first detailed survey of the country. This was to be carried out by the Army Engineering Corps. William's father had good contacts with officers of this corps and new recruits with a talent for mapping and drawing were needed. Not surprisingly, William Thomas had inherited useful skills in this area from both father and uncle and the corps took him on. The year was 1821 and William Thomas was 19 years of age.

The survey was a major project carried out mainly in the field. It began in the north, on the banks of the River Bann near Coleraine and it was there that William learned the skills of a land surveyor. He was away from home but he found the work very interesting. It brought him into contact with experienced people who helped him master the use of the geodolite, the compass, and other measuring instruments. Maps still extant show clearly his acquired mastery of map-making and calligraphy. He also had a wonderful opportunity of touring much of the north and the west of the country, its rolling landscape, hills, mountains and rivers and, more importantly, he had valuable exposure to the organisation and practices of the administration.

An important aim of the survey project was the registration of holdings and the drawing together, wherever feasible, of scattered fields to make farms more efficient. It was the first time that such a scheme, fraught as it was with difficulties, was attempted by the government. However, it was also intended to facilitate the introduction later of comparative evaluation criteria for determining rates and levies.

For six years William Thomas worked among engineers on the Ordnance Survey and in 1827, thanks largely to his aptitude and commitment, he was made assistant boundary surveyor with the responsibility of mapping out boundaries of baronies, townlands and counties. The Hydrographic Survey Office under the British Admiralty was engaged simultaneously in charting the waters around the coasts while the building of harbours and piers was the responsibility of the Board of Works, when it was established in 1831.

William Thomas and his father maintained a lively correspondence during these early years and William often sought his father's advice. William appears to have kept his father's letters and his daughter, Annabella, later privately published them. Unfortunately, none of William's letters survived.

Mulvany's early years with the Ordnance Survey involved continuous changing of abode. Starting in Coleraine, he went to Enniskillen, thence to counties Galway and Roscommon. In later years, when with the Board of Works and in charge of drainage, he resided at No. 5 Catherine Street, Limerick.

A letter from father to son reveals the close relationship between the two:

> Royal Hibernian Academy,
> 25th February 1927
>
> My Dearest William,
> If you knew the agony of mind I have endured on your account. Every day I have been picturing to myself the state of your wardrobe and every day has been a source of deepest anxiety. I know what it is to walk with an indifferent coat or hat and often have I done so ... to meet the demands of a large family, yet I could easily perceive from the averted eye or head of even an old acquaintance that an indifferent external appearance did not in their estimation entitle me to their recognition nor did even the honourable motive ... atone for the damnable error of appearing poor. ... I know from long experience how much a man's success depends upon his appearance ... I would rather have a son of mine go without his dinner than without those gentlemanly appendages ... in the absence of which genuine learning and worth are too often passed by.
>
> God bless you my darling William is the anxious wish of your affectionate father,
> Thomas J. Mulvany.

In another letter, written when William was 20 years of age, his application to his work and his desire to expand his knowledge and experience earned generous praise:

> My Dearest William,
> Why is it my darling fellow that you, possessed with such talents and with such a mind, could allow yourself to be made unhappy by the apparent want of present success. Rest assured you will very soon be deemed by your officers as one of the most useful and necessary members of the corps. Besides, you do not enter it as many others do with object in view. You merely desire to acquire that degree of knowledge which no other service you could hope to possess yourself of and having done that leave it at any time you please. Farewell my darling William and if you will but estimate yourself as I estimate you you will succeed.
> Yours, etc., etc.,
> Thomas J. Mulvany.

Yet another letter contains a certain prophetic note on William's future career:

My dearest William,

... happiness of seeing how successfully you are getting on and pain at finding myself without you on this day (December 24th). We are all unhappy at your absence but poor Mamma is breaking her heart, therefore my darling fellow proceed in the same path which you have trodden from your infancy ... truth, honour and religion, and you will enjoy the reward by being esteemed, respected and happy.

I cannot my dear William wish you a better wish than that you may be able ... to say to your son as I say to you now. I am proud of you as my son, my companion and my friend.

... I need not tell you how delighted I was at Captain Yule's interview with you, it is just as I had expected and as both Mr Johnston and Mr Temple said it would be – as to Mr Johnston I never saw him so excited as he was about you he damned a certain Captain most heartily and added 'I tell you Tom ... they have not such a lad amongst them as William, and mark my words his success will prove what I say, while other fellows will be capering about to evening parties he will be studying his profession at home in his rooms and while those caperers will be known to the country squires William shall be known to the Board of Engineers, now tell him that I said so, he is a damned sensible fellow, Tom, and you will see him at the head of his profession yet, mark my words.' Such was the verbatim opinion of our friend Johnston.

God bless you my darling fellow and send you every success,
Your affectionate father,
Thomas J. Mulvany.

Source: Mrs T. Elliott, New Zealand

At the age of 29 William married Alicia Winslow of Clogher, Co. Fermanagh, the daughter of a Catholic landowner. Her brother, Lieut Winslow of the Royal Navy, died on board HMS *Beagle*, the vessel which carried Darwin on his expedition to the Galapagos.

Their first daughter, called Eliza, was born in 1834. She died in 1849 at the age of 15. Their second daughter Alicia wrote somewhat solemn verses and some of these were later published under the title *Notes on the Journey*. Years later, one verse was carved on her headstone in the family burial plot in Düsseldorf [see p. 113].

3

William Thomas Joins the Board of Public Works

William Mulvany's progress within the Ordnance Survey was rapid. Although there is no record of formal studies or certification of his qualifications his practical experience appears to have projected him up through the ranks. In 1834, he was transferred as a civil engineer to the Board of Works. He first worked in the division responsible for inland waterways and arterial drainage. His previous experience, which had taken him all over the country, was an undoubted asset. Yet, at 28 years of age, he was comparatively young for the job.

The chairman of the Board of Works at this time was an army engineer with a remarkable career, John Fox Burgoyne (1782–1871), who had been with Wellington at Waterloo and who, having retired from the board, returned to army service at the age of 72 to serve in the Crimean War as a general and afterwards field marshal. He was the natural son of General John Burgoyne, who surrendered to American Congressional forces at the decisive Battle of Saratoga in 1777. Burgoyne and his successor, Richard Griffith are credited with laying the foundations of arterial drainage in Ireland in the first decades of the nineteenth century. Griffith was born in Hume Street, Dublin, in 1784. He was engaged in surveying and listing the bogs of Ireland as well as the Leinster coal-fields and is regarded as the father of geology in Ireland. He was knighted in 1858 and died in 1878 aged 94.

John Burgoyne took young Mulvany under his wing and was his patron during his term of office. Griffith, too, recognised Mulvany's talent, though subsequent events indicate a certain distance or, indeed, rivalry in their relations.

In the early years of the nineteenth century the rivers and inland waterways of Britain underwent rapid development as a means of transport. This happened to a lesser extent in Ireland. As Ireland had few railways, the rivers and newly constructed canals, notably the Royal and Grand Canals, were important logistical assets. The remit of the Board of Works was extended to incorporate the development of infrastructural projects such as coastal and inland harbours, fishery facilities and weirs, as well as railway works, bridges, etc. The broad aim was to improve the economic viability of the country as far as possible within limited budgets and also to relieve widespread destitution in several regions by providing work schemes for the unemployed.

One of the major plans was the drainage of the Shannon Basin and its improvement as a navigable river above its tidal reaches. The earlier construction of the two major canals from Dublin made this work a logical extension of the infrastructure. In 1835, Mulvany transferred to Limerick where his office in the Custom House overlooked the tidal river. Many of the smaller tributaries such as the Maigue, the Fergus and the Feale were to be dredged and river banks damaged by floods, refurbished. Up-country, north of Lough Derg to Shannon Harbour, similar tasks awaited his attention.

The Shannon is the longest river in Ireland with a huge catchment area embracing much of the centre of the country. If the project were to be properly tackled and there were no restraints on funding it would have been on a scale hitherto unknown in Ireland or Britain. The science of hydrology was still in its early days and experts were scarce so the corpus of experience and knowledge of arterial drainage was limited. The Board of Works engineers, given their limited resources, were pioneers in this field.

Many of the maps and task descriptions associated with this and other projects were drawn up by Mulvany. A major problem at this stage was the lack of definitive and reliable records of rainfall. It was difficult to foresee whether works carried out, such as the raising of dykes, would, in fact, withstand exceptional flooding. Today, it is difficult to perceive how the regulation of rivers was carried out at all, with the primitive technical means at the disposal of these men.

As well as the technical and organisational nature of his work, Mulvany was also required to draft proposals for legislation governing the navigation of the Shannon and to enable drainage works to begin. The Acts 5 and 6 Vict. C.89 were the first Acts of Parliament to be passed by Westminster for this purpose. There was close liaison between Mulvany and Burgoyne during this period and nothing was done without prior permission of the secretary of the treasury, Sir Charles Trevelyan, in London. Mulvany, still in his thirties, travelled to London frequently for consultations. In those days travellers could leave Dublin on the night mail steamer, be in London early next morning and return that same night to Dublin. Travelling throughout Ireland, on the other hand, especially where a coach and four was necessary, was less convenient and more time-consuming.

About this time, the use of clay pipes to drain low-lying but fertile land began. The system had been tried with success in England. Because of its length, depth and often leisurely rate of flow in normal seasons, the Shannon was an ideal waterway for inland navigation. The Royal and Grand Canals, built in 1770–74, connected Dublin port with the midlands and then with the tidal port of Limerick in the mid-west. At first horse-drawn barges were used and later steam-propelled vessels.

It was then possible to travel overnight from Portobello in Dublin to the River Shannon at Shannon Harbour, near Banagher. Some of these express services were known as 'fly boats'. (A century later real flying boats connected Foynes on the Estuary with Botwood in Newfoundland and Lisbon as well as Southampton.) In one of his letters, William's father describes a trip he made on one of the canal vessels to Shannon Harbour and Roscommon to execute a commission that he described as very enjoyable and convivial. During the nineteenth century and well into the late 1940s these canals continued to be used for the transport of general cargoes, particularly grain and stout.

The first laws governing the navigation of the River Shannon were passed in 1839. In a number of reports and memoranda leading up to this, Mulvany made a significant contribution to the future management of the river facilities. These plans also embraced the construction of fish weirs. A commission was appointed to supervise the use of the river and Mulvany was appointed District Engineer. He had a large staff working for him which included his youngest brother, Thomas John, also an engineer, and his nephew, John Latimer.

Apart from work on the Shannon and canals – his remit covered the estuary to Loop Head – Mulvany was also involved in planning and supervising road construction. His executive functions brought him into daily contact with land and property owners, builders, contractors and hauliers over a wide area. Much of the work was contracted out to local firms and he also liaised with urban councils, contractors and trades people at all levels and interpreted their needs and wishes to the board in Dublin and through it, the treasury in London.

In the late eighteenth century, there were plans for a canal to link the river Erne with the Shannon and provide the northern province of Ulster with a water-borne connection for barges to the tidal reaches of the Shannon at Limerick. Goods from the industrialised north could then be transported relatively cheaply and easily to ships sailing between the port of Limerick and North America.

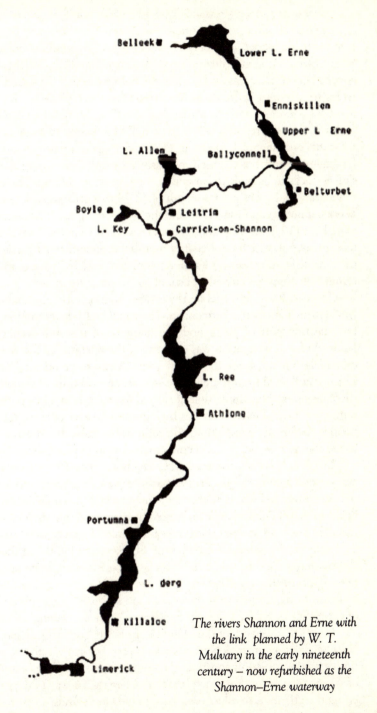

The rivers Shannon and Erne with the link planned by W. T. Mulvany in the early nineteenth century – now refurbished as the Shannon–Erne waterway

Preliminary surveys revealed that advantage could be taken of the lakes in an almost direct line between the Shannon near Leitrim town and Upper Lough Erne near Belturbet. These were Lough Scur, St John's Lough, Kilbardon Lough, Lough Garadice, Ballymagovern Lough, Derrycassan Lough and Coologue Lough. Three different routes were under discussion. However, these plans lay dormant for decades. In 1839, Mulvany, then 33 years, was entrusted with the task of preparing a survey as well as a feasibility study on the canal's commercial potential. He decided upon a route to link Ballynamore and Ballyconnell, prepared all maps, drawings of the sluices, locks to be built in cut and dressed limestone blocks. There were two canals over a total length of 62.7 km with sixteen locks. Work commenced in June 1846 and the cost of the project was estimated at £110,301. Thousands of manual workers were employed in its construction which resulted in substantial economic relief during the terrible Famine years. It was not completed until 1859 due to intermittent stoppages caused by lack of government finance.

The canal was to be operated by trustees nominated by the counties Leitrim, Cavan and Fermanagh. The canal had a dual function, i.e., the transport of goods and the drainage of the surrounding lands. As far as navigation was concerned, the operational life was extremely limited, from 1860 until 1869. A not-so-grand total of £18 was collected from the eight vessels which paid tolls, although there may have been more that neglected to pay tolls. It was a poor return for a canal eventually costing almost a quarter of a million pounds. Before its completion, the railways in Ireland had established themselves as a fast and convenient means of transport.

In 1994, however, the waterway, which was derelict for over a century and a half, was modernised to serve the leisure sports industry. A substantial cross-border programme of works was undertaken by the Office of Public Works to deepen the fairway, rebuild the locks, install sluice gates and refurbish the canal banks. The total cost was £15 million and was subvented by the EU Regional Fund and the International Fund for Ireland. Nowadays, tourists from home and overseas enjoy the scenic beauty of the canal and Lough Erne region. Mulvany's original plans for the project are archived in the library of the Office of Public Works in St Stephen's Green, Dublin.

In 1829, ownership of the Shannon, from Limerick to Killaloe, was vested in the Limerick Navigation Company but in 1831, the authority for ensuring and controlling navigation passed to the Board of Works. The primary aim now was to regulate the fairway by deepening the channels to allow passage to fully-laden vessels, with the secondary aim of repairing the river banks and draining riparian lands. The 1835 Act of Parliament empowered the commissioners to enter land and undertake any works considered necessary. Any claims for damage to property, weirs or mills had to be presented to the board and it was empowered to take final and binding decisions regarding any claims for compensation.

In the spring of 1839, severe flooding took place which badly damaged many of the works then in progress. Some of the many small mill owners, whose grinding machinery was water-driven, had to close down due to the new regulation of the rivers or changes in the water levels. A system of compensation to deal with such cases was introduced and was administered by Mulvany and his department. Thus, Mulvany found himself involved not only in the technical and administrative aspects of individual projects in different locations but also in the legal intricacies of dealing with proprietors of small or cottage industries.

John Fox Burgoyne (1782–1871), chairman of Board of Works Later knighted, General and Field Marshal

Sir Richard Griffith (1784–1878), another chairman of the Board of Works

4

Appointed Assistant Commissioner in 1842

In 1842, the functions and scope of the Board of Works in Ireland increased significantly. Mulvany, having distinguished himself in the field, was appointed assistant commissioner at 44 years of age. Harry D. Jones was the other commissioner and Richard Griffith was chairman at this time, having succeeded Sir John Burgoyne. Griffith, who was later knighted, was an eminent geologist and was the first to explore and charter the natural resources of Ireland. Mulvany was in charge of arterial drainage for the whole country but the following year was given the additional responsibility for Fisheries. His salary was £600 and he operated from headquarters in Dublin. New drainage plans were drawn up for other rivers in Ireland, notably the Blackwater, the Suir, the Nore and the Barrow.

Trevelyan, who was assistant secretary to the Treasury for 16 years, later outlined the origin of this new legislation:

> Sir John Burgoyne, with the assistance of Mr Mulvany, brought to bear upon the extended project of arterial drainage all over Ireland the important experience acquired in the execution of the great Shannon Works and upon that foundation the Act of 5 and 6 Vict. C.89 was based.

The flooding of 1839, and insufficiently protected river banks led to large tracts of low-lying land with good soil being lost to agriculture. Another militating factor was the tentative nature of some works, often caused by lack of central funding from London. These large wetlands, together with frost, compounded the problem of the potato failure a few years later.

The problem of flooding needed to be tackled on a national scale and the first report covering drainage and inland fisheries was published in 1840; eleven reports were issued, the last in 1850. During this time Mulvany travelled to London frequently for planning and budgetary conferences. From 1846, loans were granted to landowners wishing to carry out their own drainage works. Private contractors were usually employed on the board's own projects. Mulvany supported this policy as he was convinced it would provide a useful economic component to the locality, instead of engaging gangs of travelling workers following projects far away from their homes and families.

A sizeable part of the rural population was engaged in either inland or coastal fishing, although for many this was only a part-time occupation as it was governed by seasonality. Stretches of the longer rivers, such as the Shannon, the Corrib and the Blackwater, provided fishermen with an income which was generally above that of the labourer or farm worker. Landowners with riparian rights, i.e., rights to land on a river bank, employed water bailiffs to patrol the rivers but poaching was common and the courts were kept busy. In the 1830s, there had been over-fishing and lack of respect for closed seasons and in the following years, there were lower catches and many fishermen lost their livelihood. Under Mulvany, new stringent regulations to enforce by-laws and control indiscriminate fishing were introduced.

New fishing weirs for salmon and eels were constructed or rehabilitated at Corbally, near Limerick, and near the rapids at Castleconnell and on Lough Derg. A stake weir was placed across the River Laune in Kerry as well as a slob weir for eels. Fish passes were installed and during the breeding season most work on the river banks was suspended to avoid interference.

At the same time work began on improving facilities for coastal fisheries. A number of fish-curing stations and salting facilities were set up all around the coast for curing herring and mackerel which were exported to England, the continent and America. Practically all of the fishing vessels were small, open or half-decked boats, unsuitable for venturing far from the shore, but as there were so many of them thousands of families were supported by fishing for at least part of the year. In the latter half of the nineteenth century, cargoes of salted herring from Dingle, Baltimore and Dunmore East found their way to the mid-west of America where they were the staple diet of Chinese coolies and Irish labourers building America's railroads.

When John Peel was elected prime minister for the second time, he chose Sir Philip Grey as viceroy in Dublin and Lord Eliot as chief secretary. Eliot had been with the Scottish Board of Fisheries before that and took a particular interest in the development of this sector when he came to Ireland. At his instigation, Mulvany gave a number of lectures in Dublin on the fisheries in general and their potential for expansion.

The two Mulvany brothers became prominent officials of the administration. They were both members of the Institution of Civil

Engineers in Ireland. On 11 March 1851, Thomas John delivered an important lecture to the institute while his elder brother was in the chair. He described a system for de-watering works using an improvised screw pump that could be driven by manual effort or by using horses. This interest in pumps was in the subsequent careers of the two brothers.

As a member of the Institution of Civil Engineers in Ireland, W. T. Mulvany read five papers before its members. These were:

> Observations on Regulating Weirs (1845)
> Drainage and Improvement of Ballytigue Lough (1845)
> An Account of the Proposed Balance Gates and Regulating Weirs for Lough Erne (1848)
> On the Ballytigue Drainage Works (1848)
> On Facts Connected with the Costs of Blasting Operations (1848).

His brother, Thomas John, read three papers:

> On the Drainage of the Turloughs in Co. Roscommon (1848)
> On the Use of Self-Registering Rain and Flood Gauges (1851)
> On the Use of Screw Pumps for Unwatering Works (1851).

On these three occasions the elder brother was in the chair.

Mulvany was engaged in plans for the development of the River Bann to meet the needs of increased shipping. In Portrush a fishing port was set up and efforts were made to spread the costs of this among local authorities in the hinterland as secondary beneficiaries of the project. Mulvany supported this arrangement for financing the project against very strong opposition. As in the arterial drainage schemes there was lobbying at the political level to influence the execution of some of the board's plans.

At this time, many new roads and bridges were under construction. Mulvany was enamoured of the system of lifting and swivel bridges then in use on the continent. One swivel bridge section on the originally named Wellesley Bridge (now Sarsfield Bridge) over the Shannon in Limerick was in use for the best part of a century.

By this time, the Mulvany family had moved back from Limerick to Dublin. They first lived at Dundrum Lodge and later at Dirker Lodge, Cross Ave., Booterstown.

William Thomas Mulvany in his 50s

T. J. Mulvany, brother of William T. Mulvany

Thomas Robert Mulvany, son of William T. Mulvany

5

The Plight of Tenants and Rural Workers

In the northern province of Ulster with its predominantly Protestant population, farmers were protected against wilful eviction. This right did not exist in the other provinces. In the south, forceful eviction of tenant farmers was an all too common occurrence and fanned the flames of discord – acts of terrorism against the landed gentry were frequent. Many of the landowners only came over from England during the fox-hunting season. Oscar Wilde later described them as 'the unspeakable chasing the uneatable'.

During previous generations the distribution of land did not properly support a population of about 8 million. Emigration to England, Scotland, Canada, America and Australia was common. Most parents raised families only to see them depart for foreign shores, never to return. As well as hunger and poverty, this anguish at the loss of beloved sons and daughters, the very cream of the country's youth, stalked the land. The future held out little hope of relief and apathy and fatalism became ingrained.

Sir John Burgoyne commented:

> A family in the west of Ireland was considered provided for, if once located on from one to three or four acres of land; a cabin could be raised in a few days without the expense of a sixpence, the potatoes at the cost of very little labour, supplied them with a sufficiency of food, with which, from habit, they were perfectly content, and a pig, or with some, a cow, a donkey, or pony, and occasional labour at a very low rate of wages, gave them what was necessary to pay a rent, and for such clothing and other articles as were absolutely necessary, and which with a greater proportion were on the lowest scale of human existence.

Friedrich Engels (1820–1895) from Wuppertal and supporter of Karl Marx, then living in England, observed Irish immigrants in Manchester and described them harshly:

> These people, virtually brought up without civilisation, used to going without from youth, raw, fond of drink, not caring for the children, come over and bring their brutal ways into a class of the English population that truly has little wish for education and morality.
>
> (*Die Lage der arbeitenden Klassen in England*, Leipzig 1845)

This judgment did not prevent Engels from taking a Galway girl, Mary Burns, as his mistress, and, when she died, her sister Lizzie.[1]

The report of the Poor Law Commission in 1837 revealed that, out of a population of 8.5 million, 585,000 heads of families were destitute and 2,300,000 were dependent on public or private charity in order to survive and 27% of the population were deemed paupers.

While considering the social and economic state of Ireland at this time it is well to remember that in most townlands, especially in the west, the north-west and the south, Irish was the language spoken by the adult population in the home and the language was yet another barrier between rich and poor. Charles Trevelyan was appointed assistant secretary to the Treasury in 1840 and under him relief schemes for the unemployed and destitute were undertaken, beginning in 1845. In each local district, relief committees were set up and funded by the government and local councils to provide cooked meals – these were known as soup kitchens.

The new relief works were mainly aimed at providing work. Mulvany invested considerable effort into recruiting labourers to carry out useful construction work on roads, rivers and canals. In County Clare alone, there were 25,000 working on projects directed by him. Many boundary walls were built then and some of the mountain roads are still in use today.

The plight of the rural population was even worse when the potato crop failed in 1846 and 1847. By the middle of the eighteenth century, potatoes were the staple diet of the people. When the blight spread rapidly, no alternative was found or sought and the problem escalated out of control. Almost two million people died within two years and in the beginning the true extent of the devastation was not recognised by the government in London.

The first report of the potato disease in Europe was recorded near Hanover in 1830 and there was an outbreak in Nova Scotia and New England in 1842. In August 1845, it was first reported in the Isle of Wight and later in Kent. The disease was also reported in Belgium.

Father Theobald Matthew, founder of the Temperance Movement in Ireland, wrote:

> On the 27th of last month I passed from Cork to Dublin and this doomed (potato) plant blooms in all the luxuriance of an abundant harvest. Returning on the 3rd inst. I beheld with sorrow one wide waste

---

[1] *'The news of Mary's death surprised as well as crushed us. She was good and witty and was so devoted to you.' Letter from Marx to Engels, 8 Jan. 1863.*

of putrefying vegetation. In many places the wretched people were seated on the fences of their decaying gardens, wringing their hands and wailing bitterly the destruction that left them foodless.

When the full horror of the potato blight became known landowners as well as the London *Times* sought to deny the seriousness of the situation. There had been some crop failures due to unfavourable weather before 1845 in Ireland but in the following year indications were that a major portion of the crop, if not all, would be lost. John Peel, the then British prime minister, had been forewarned of the dire consequences and secretly made arrangements to ship Indian meal from the United States to Ireland. The secrecy was dictated by the desire not to upset importers and merchants whose markets might be affected and because the government in London had no similar precedent for such a humanitarian action that might be construed as an interference in trade. This policy of *laissez-faire* marked the thinking of many British governments then and later.

This Indian meal was distributed to depots set up under government control around the country and sold at one penny per pound to the starving population. However, there were not enough supplies available nor were the mechanics of transport and distribution adequate to the occasion. The meal was unsuitable; in America, it was fed to hogs and, being difficult to grind, it was difficult to digest and was known as 'Peel's brimstone'.

The Famine ruptured the body and soul of the Irish as a community and those who could, left Ireland. They left a void which some commentators feel was never filled. In 1847, some supplies of corn were imported from America to be sold to the starving people. Marcus Goodbody, a prominent miller and Quaker, said it was ridiculous to try to sell corn to people who had no money to pay for it and that it should be distributed free.

Another problem to compound the situation of chaos and misery that gripped Ireland in 1846 was the fact that most of the rural population had little idea of the value of money. Work on the land was often paid for by barter in potatoes or vegetables or meat or amounts deducted from rents owed. Many tenants paid rents by growing oats or wheat and some went hungry with oats and wheat stored for the day the rent was due. The barter system meant that when the crops failed all was lost.

The following June, the Whigs defeated the Tories in London and Lord John Russell became prime minister. At harvest time the blight was evident for the second season, only more widespread.

Russell decided that no government emergency rations would be purchased. He, too, was not prepared to risk the anger of corn merchants by interfering in the markets.

A new scheme was devised to make ratepayers pay for the relief works spread over the following ten years at an interest of 3%. The committees came up with ridiculous schemes on the basis that those ten years were an eternity away. The Board of Works was responsible for vetting these schemes. Mulvany and his two fellow commissioners tried to ensure that only useful operations would be undertaken and he criticised the building of useless roads and the digging of drains which were subsequently filled in again.

Estimates of the population based on church returns were:

1801	5,395,465	1851	6,552,385
1821	6,801,827	1871	5,412,377
1841	8,175,124	1881	5,174,386.

The decrease in the population from 1841 onwards reflects the extent of the disaster and this decline continued well into the twentieth century.

6

1847 – Effects of Famine

Early in 1847, Mulvany went to London to plead with Treasury officials for more significant and more generous financial support in carrying out the many relief projects then under way. He remained there for several weeks, keeping up the pressure with several government departments.

During the preceding months, he and his fellow commissioners as well as the entire staff of the board were engaged in crisis management of unheard of dimensions. Griffith and Mulvany travelled all over the country, often at night to save time. Mulvany's father had died in 1845 and it would appear that he took a long time to get over this loss. The hard work and the extensive travel began to take its toll on his health.

For anyone in a responsible administrative position at that time the spectre of hunger and misery throughout the country can only have led not to mere frustration but to anger as well. In hindsight, many commentators agree that the worst effects of the Famine could have been avoided. Westminster did not do all in its power to ameliorate the suffering and pain, not because of lack of will but, rather, through lack of experience and competence in dealing with this extraordinary catastrophe. The law and vested interests allowed corn to be imported into Ireland and re-exported past corpses lying on the streets. This was typical of the *laissez-faire* approach which successive British governments adopted in relation to traders and merchants over many years.

At this time, the benefits of the industrial revolution were being felt in mainland Britain. The construction of railways, many of them in private ownership, had expanded enormously. People who had seldom travelled no further than a horse or coach could bring them in a day were suddenly able to travel 80 miles and more in one day. This factor made a tremendous difference to trade and commerce.

Although the first railways in Ireland between Dublin and Kingstown (Dun Laoghaire) had been opened in 1834, in the following eight years only 123 miles of track had been laid. There appears to have been little private capital available in Ireland to emulate the example set in England. Railways were considered a highly speculative adventure.

In England, the development of the railways went hand in hand with the development of coal-mining. By 1840, there were 2,000 miles of track in use but by 1848, this had grown to 5,000 miles.

> In the forties, under the less scrupulous leadership of George Hudson, the 'Railway King', the general public plunged headlong into the speculation of the 'railway mania' and lost much money on bogus or unsuccessful companies. But henceforth the normal way of transporting heavy goods and the normal way of travelling was by rail.
> (*English Social History*, G. M. Trevelyan)

Mulvany was more inclined to support the establishment of state-owned railways. He was aware that speculative capital was not readily available in Ireland to set up a viable system. He examined the matter closely and determined that the cost could vary enormously from £10,000 to £80,000 per mile of track. Nonetheless, he took a close interest in the manner in which this part of the infrastructure was progressing in England, and, at a later juncture in his career, he had a lot to say on this subject.

My Lords also advert to their Minute of 4th October 1842, in which they approved of the appointment of Mr Wm. T. Mulvany to be one of the Inspectors of Fisheries under the Act of 6 Vict. c. 106, with a salary of £200 per annum, he being at the same time appointed a commissioner of Drainage with a salary of £400 per annum, and Mr Mulvany having been recommended to my Lords by the Chief Secretary for Ireland as the person best qualified, by his zeal and activity and intimate acquaintance with the details of the Irish Fisheries, for the appointment of commissioner of Fisheries, my Lords are pleased to direct that a warrant be prepared for their signature, in conformity with the provisions of the first section of the Act of 8 & 9 Vict. c. 108, constituting and appointing William T. Mulvany, Esq. to be a commissioner of Fisheries to assist the commissioners appointed under the Royal Sign Manual, by virtue of Act of 1 & 2 Will. 4 for the Extension and Promotion of Public Works in Ireland, who are by the second section of the Act 5 & 6 Vict. c. 106 constituted Commissioners of Fisheries under that Act.

Transmit copy of this Minute to the Commissioners of Public Works in Ireland for their information, and desire they will submit to my Lords, in conformity with the provisions of the Act of 5 & 6 Vict. c. 106, the name of such person as they may consider best qualified to succeed Mr Mulvany as Inspector of Fisheries, for their Lordships' approval.

At the same time, acquaint them that before the estimates to be submitted to Parliament next Session are prepared, my Lords will consider what salary it will be proper to allow Mr Mulvany as commissioner of Fisheries, in addition to his salary of £400 per annum as commissioner of Drainage, and what salary it will be proper to allow to his successor as Inspector of Fisheries.

Transmit copy of this Minute to Sir T. Freemantle, for the information of the Lord Lieutenant of Ireland.

The Commissioner of Public Works to Mr TREVELYAN: December 6, 1845.

A vacancy having occurred for an inspector of Fisheries by the appointment of Mr Mulvany to be a commissioner of Fisheries, and, in pursuance of your Lordships' instructions, we have to recommend Mr William J. Ffennell to be an inspector. The appointment to be considered temporary, the same having been explained to that gentleman. Mr Mulvany's salary was only £200, in consequence of his receiving £400 as an Assistant Commissioner for Drainage. We therefore submit, for your Lordships' consideration, that Mr Ffennell's salary should be fixed at £300 per annum, the same as the other Inspector is now receiving.

Treasury Minute on the above – 12 December 1845

The above is an extract of Treasury Minutes noting W. T. Mulvany's appointment as commissioner of Fisheries

7

Aftermath of the Famine

Not only were the people sufferering the aftermath of the Famine, many of the landlords were left with meagre financial reserves and some of them blamed their plight on the government and the Board of Works.

The improvement of riparian property was enjoyed mainly by the landowners. To finance operations preliminary surveys had to be funded by them and were carried out by the Board of Works. These surveys were usually approved by two of the board's commissioners. A majority of two-thirds of the owners of any lands affected by a proposed scheme would be required to give their assent before the commencement of the project. There was also provision for final approval at a later stage when the estimates were complete. Initial capital was raised by the board either in the form of private loans or by advances from the Treasury. Repayment was by means of a levy on improved lands at a stipulated rate per acre, spread over a number of years.

However, the system was fraught with problems. Either the landlords delayed giving assent or simply refused it or the Treasury delayed transferring the necessary funds in time to start or continue the work. Such delays, and they were frequent, exposed half-finished works to the elements and it was not unusual for Mulvany to see works begun in the autumn destroyed by winter flooding.

These problems were so severe that a Summary Proceedings Act was introduced in March 1846 to short-circuit bureaucratic impediments or delays in carrying out relief schemes in land drainage at the onset of the Famine. This legislation enabled the board, and through it, Mulvany, to undertake drainage operations without second assents from the landlords, a provision about which landowners were either unaware or had overlooked the consequences of. When the final costs of a number of these works became known it was clear that some would considerably exceed the original estimates.

Several landowners took issue with the Board of Works. One of the vociferous critics was William Parsons, third Earl of Rosse of Birr Castle, Co. Offaly, whose lands bordered the River Brosna along which serious flooding had occurred repeatedly. The river is a major tributary of the Shannon and the riparian lands are good for crops and grazing.

The third Earl of Rosse who held a hereditary seat in the House of Lords was born in 1800 and died in 1867. He was a man of considerable talent, being a self-educated engineer. His family opposed the Act of Union with England and he supported Daniel O'Connell's successful campaign for Catholic Emancipation. Of the many achievements in his lifetime perhaps those in the field of astronomy are the most important. He designed and built what became for 75 years the largest telescope in the world on the grounds of Birr Castle. It was 50 feet long and 7 feet wide. By means of this large telescope the lens of which was ground and polished on the site, many galaxies of the heavens were first seen and recorded. Birr became known to astronomers throughout the world and many came to visit Birr. The remains have been restored recently and are seen by many thousands of visitors to the castle and its unique gardens every year.

Statue of Third Earl of Rosse, Birr

He was conferred with the Order of St Patrick by Queen Victoria and was president of the Royal Society and chancellor of Dublin University. A bronze statue in his memory was erected in the main square of Birr ten years after his death. Despite the independence and 'Irishness' of the Parsons family Lord Rosse had very close relations with political and administrative leaders in London. (William Parsons' son, Sir Charles Parsons, OM, KCB, became an even more prominent engineer and is credited with the invention of the steam turbine which, by utilising higher pressure, became the main propulsion system for shipping in the nineteenth and twentieth centuries.)

In his confrontation with the Board of Works, the third earl took full advantage of his political contacts in Britain. He realised that his principal adversary within the board was Mulvany in his capacity of commissioner in charge of drainage. He had long discussions with some of Mulvany's engineers in the field who reported back on the very angry attitude the earl had taken on the issue of costs for drainage works on his lands and on his not being adequately consulted in advance.

He then rallied for support by other landowners in Ireland and agitated for the setting up of a select committee of the House of Lords to enquire into the Board of Works' operations in Ireland. The committee was set up and its twenty-three members comprised: The Lord Privy Seal (Marquess of Salisbury), the Marquess of Lansdowne, the Marquess of Bath, the Marquess of Normandy, the Earl of Derby, the Earl of Sandwich, the Earl of Essex, the Earl of Albermarle, the Earl of Clarendon, the Earl of Talbot, the Earl of Wicklow, the Earl of Lucan, the Earl of Nelson, the Earl of Harrowby, the Earl of Glanville, Viscount Hutchinson, Lord Rosse, Lord Beaumont, Lord Polwirth, Lord Dinever, Lord Wodehouse, Lord Sommerville, Lord Monteagle of Brandon. Only seven of these peers had estates in Ireland. Lord Rosse was the chairman.

The gravamen of the complaint was that the board, and specifically Mulvany, had forced the government to spend three million pounds on drainage works which they, the landlords, had not approved of in advance and that the scheme had been unduly prolonged at their expense. Additionally, they complained, the original estimates were far below the actual costs of the works.

The additional costs about which Rosse and his friends complained would not have amounted to more than two years' rental of the lettings in his case, and there is little doubt that the works were not only necessary but they most certainly secured and improved the land. During the previous two years, there had been a veritable clamour by many bodies such as the Royal Agricultural Society for drainage schemes throughout the country and hundreds of individual petitions were made to the government in this connection. The Board of Works was merely responding positively to a widespread demand.

But there was much more behind Lord Rosse's campaign. The big landowners in Ireland, because of their property and wealth, exercised an almost feudal right and influence over tenants, Church and State and political life. Little could be done without their approval and support.

On 11 April, 1852, the Board of Works engineer, William Barry of Ferbane District, wrote a letter to Mulvany:

... You are aware of the intended parliamentary investigations ...

> When in Tullamore I heard a great deal about it from members of the Grand Jury ... among them some intimate acquaintances they were totally unreserved in their remarks. What surprised me most was the feeling against yourself. To you ... is attributed the alleged twisting and turning of the Acts ... a variety of charges which would puzzle you to understand ... I now find a well organised plan ... Yesterday I call on Lord Ross (sic) and had long conversation ... the matter will be ... in the Lords ... early next week and if the session lasts long enough the intended investigation will be had before its close.
>
> The remodelling of the Act will be the general object giving the Proprietor ... control of the works ... but there will be a special attack against yourself its object being your removal from your present position. It is not meant to interfere with ... the board but to have in your place 'an Engineer of experience' ... probably some English engineer – to remove you they are determined and every species of influence will be brought to bear ... they expect some strange revelations in respect to some parties employed by the board ... and that you would not come quite clear of having your favour to be purchased.
>
> *Larcom Mss., Letter No. 71, National Library of Ireland*

The chairman of the Board of Works, Richard Griffith, was in London on 22 April 1850, for a meeting with Sir Charles Trevelyan and the chancellor of the exchequer. In a letter to his deputy, Major Thomas A. Larcom (later general) Griffith wrote:

> Trevelyan enquired closely as to my opinion of Mulvany's honesty in regard to receiving bribes or appointments, I told him I thought him perfectly honest, that he had appointed his own near connexions but that I thought them all clever men and suited to the positions in which they were placed: he then asked was I certain his engineers and assistants did not sell places I said I thought not, that I had never heard a surmise to that effect but that I could not vouch that that had never occurred.
>
> It is evident that both Sir C. Wood and Trevelyan understand Mulvany's character as well as we do and I feel certain that if he does not cordially assist in arranging matters that they will not retain him. You will judge yourself from what I have said how matters stand.
>
> *Larcom Mss, Letter No. 54, National Library of Ireland.*

Mulvany was shocked at the news of the decision to hold an enquiry. He set about assembling all the relevant documents, petitions and correspondence pertaining to the 121 drainage projects within the entire scheme. On only eleven of these were works held in abeyance awaiting final assents from landowners under the Summary Proceedings Act that was intended to cut out unnecessary delays and give additional powers to the board. The total cost on all works, including the over-runs on original estimates, averaged £5 14s 7d. per acre. Over 17,000 workers were employed on these works.

At that time the status of the big house in Ireland was under attack through increasing costs of the aristocratic life, the growing wealth of industrialists, some of whom may not have been deemed gentlemen, and in a much more significant way by the power won by the higher levels of public administration. The days of the landowners' absolute authority were numbered. Lord Rosse knew he was taking on a lot by attacking the Board of Works and through it the Treasury.

On the principle of *divide et impera* the committee criticised Mulvany personally. His competence and suitability for the position was questioned and the line of questioning may have played on internal rivalry that may well have existed between the chairman, Griffith, and Mulvany. When things did come to a head Griffith's defence of his fellow commissioner was less than staunch.

Lord Rosse, as chairman, examined a number of witnesses including Trevelyan, the chief government official responsible. He vigorously defended the additional costs involved in many of the projects and pointed out that by law it was not necessary to secure assents in all cases.

The Summary Proceedings Act was designed to give the board powers to go ahead with works and it remained open whether, once original assents had been obtained, it should consult again with the landowners when additional costs became necessary. Throughout the hearing there was a line of questioning aimed at undermining the board's interpretation of this legislation on the basis that it was high-handed and ignored the financial interests of the proprietors of the land, who, it was vehemently suggested, were best equipped to manage their own estates.

The questions directly and indirectly concerned Mulvany's competence and experience. Before the enquiry, Trevelyan had asked Griffith about Mulvany's probity in the case of appointments and Griffith assured him of his complete confidence in his colleague and that, if some relatives or friends had secured positions, it was solely on their suitability and very high qualifications.

The chairman put it to Trevelyan and other witnesses that before the commencement of these works Mulvany should have sought the advice of other eminent authorities and experts abroad. The chairman seemed to overlook the fact that the drainage operation on the Shannon and its tributaries was the greatest single operation of its kind in the Ireland and British Isles. Nothing on this scale had been attempted in England and the experience gained was setting precedents in the science of hydrology.

In his statement Trevelyan said:

> That great work was ably carried through and in my opinion was perfectly successful ... it cleared people's heads and enabled them to understand the subject ... it became apparent that the drainage of bogs ... which had always been the great object in former days was not the primary object, that the really important thing was to open the channels of the rivers, the main outfalls of the country. The first effect of his is to improve the adjoining lands ... to valuable pastures and meadows. The second is to furnish deep and clear arteries ... which will allow thorough drainage to be carried out all over the country and a third object what has always been considered the first, the gradual drainage of the bogs which no doubt may be reclaimed to a certain extent ... the borders and more manageable parts of them ... but the complete drainage of the bogs extends far into the future and a great proportion of them will be more valuable as peat than for any other purpose to supply fuel to future generations.

The next witness was Richard Griffith, chairman of the board and successor to John Fox Burgoyne. The eminent geologist, born in Hume Street, was the first to explore and chart the natural resources of Ireland. In reply to close questioning, he stoutly defended the additional expenditure on some of the works. However, he pointed out that had he been in charge he would have consulted the landowners before proceeding. This admission was hardly helpful to Mulvany's case and revealed Griffith's desire not to continue on a confrontational course.

The third witness, Major Thomas Larcom, deputy chairman of the board, was the *eminence grise* behind the Ordnance Survey. Although a professional engineer and an Englishman by birth, he was appointed on a committee for the transcription and translation of the Brehon Laws, the ancient legal system in Ireland. In his evidence, he gave great appreciation to the work of Mulvany and his magnificent conception of his drainage project. The chairman asked him whether Mulvany had wielded the sole charge of the department and he replied: 'He has had the sole charge'. Asked whether the general work of supervision was executed by Mulvany, he replied: 'It was, by dint of great personal labour'. Questioned about the total costs he said:

> I think it will present to Europe the most extraordinary work of the

kind ever done by private parties and at a cheap cost. If £800 per mile excavates these rivers and if you find that the cheapest railway executed in Ireland, the Galway line, amounts to £3,000–£4,000 a mile for earthworks alone, in dry land, cutting out of a hill and filling up a valley, certainly the result cannot be otherwise than that on the whole these drainages have been cheap beyond all measure.

Larcom also explained the problems relating to funding:

> It was just at the time of the total want of money in the country. We could not borrow on any terms then. But in justice to Mr Mulvany, it is only fair to state, when one looks at these works, that they present the boldest and most vigorous scheme of drainage and however irregularly they may have been carried out from difficulties as to funds yet they exhibit an amount of engineering talent, boldness of conception and vigour of execution which is one of the most extraordinary things on record.

When Mulvany was called to give evidence, it was obvious that he had prepared himself thoroughly beforehand. He had all relevant data with him but preferred to be questioned orally on any aspects the committee wished. In a sense, it must have been humiliating for a man who had worked hard and diligently, who had been exposed to the plight of destitute people during the Famine and who had been moved to do all in his power to alleviate distress. Here he was called to defend himself within the gilded chambers of Westminster, and the chairman confronting him was the chief complainant.

At first, he was closely questioned on the history of his employment with the Board of Works and previously with the Ordnance Survey. Then he was asked whether he felt he could exercise control over the drainage department without being materially interfered with by the other members of the Board of Works and he replied:

> No, mine is departmental duty, performed in concurrence with the whole board. The general principles of everything are settled with the whole board and I carry out the departmental duty of the drainage, the fisheries, etc.

Asked whether he would refer to the board before recommending, for instance, a subordinate officer, he replied:

> The appointment of every subordinate officer is approved by me after I have considered the case; it is then considered by the chairman and sanctioned by him, and as to a certain class of appointment, which we

call staff, it goes over to the Treasury and must receive their approval before it is carried out under present arrangements.

He then made a very long oral statement outlining the history of arterial drainage in Ireland which began in the eighteenth century. In all, lands belonging to 3,100 landowners were drained. He himself had been responsible for drainage for over ten years. He explained at length the complexities of planning and executing works on land that was subject to regular flooding, the provisions of the relevant legislation, the liaison with the landowners and the drawing up of contracts with private parties for the execution of the works under the board's supervision, as well as the securing of funds from the Treasury, private loans or by levies on the landowners whose lands had been improved. He adverted to the delays, sometimes up to two years, in commencing some works mostly due to the lack of initial funding and the dilatoriness of some landlords in giving their assent. He supported this by referring to the 'resolutions of the Royal Agricultural Society and the subscribers to the Fergus Drainage and many letters pressing the government to make the legislation more compulsory to take whole measures into their hands and to proceed with them for the purpose of affording immediate employment of a useful nature.'

The committee tried to nail Mulvany on the question of the second assents. Past legislation made it incumbent on the board to procure final agreement before proceeding with works. What the committee members did not, or would not, understand was that subsequent legislation empowered the board to go ahead without further consultations with the proprietors if they felt necessary.

Under questioning Mulvany proved himself totally informed regarding the articles relevant to the situation but also with their practical applications on the ground. The committee had intended to hear him on one day only but so exhaustive was his evidence and so vigorous was his defence of the board that it decided to afford him a second day in which to present his case. He realised that he was up against formidable opponents and that even with the law on his side the makers of the law would have the last word.

In its report the select committee went to great pains to find fault with the board and, in particular with Mulvany, notwithstanding the fact that it admitted that the landowners were favourable to 'half measures' and 'whether the proprietors were right, or whether, on the other hand, the officer in charge of the drainage department of the board was right is a question upon which the committee are unable to offer any opinion. This, however, seems probable, that had the wishes of the proprietors been ascertained previously to any large departure from the plans and estimates originally agreed upon, there would have been a very general dissent.'

The committee seems to have totally ignored the important secondary aim of the projects, namely the alleviation of distress during and after the Famine. Its members, at least some of them, were complainants with vested interests as well as judges and jurors in the case. The select committee lost little time in reaching its conclusions.

The Treasury was strongly censured for failing to protect the rights of the landowners. For Trevelyan this was very serious and it weighed heavily with him. However, he remained a further seven years in office. Lord Rosse's committee criticised the Board of Works for not seeking the advice of eminent engineers in other countries. It overlooked the fact that the pioneering work of the board's engineers, especially in the Shannon drainage yielded knowledge and experience not available hitherto.

In this connection it is interesting to draw attention to a paper written by Prof. James Dooge in 1957 and presented to a section of the British Association for the Advancement of Science meeting in Dublin, entitled 'The Rational Method for Estimating Flood Peaks', in which he showed that the rudiments of this method were laid by Mulvany himself, they were improved upon by a number of his engineers and perfected in a brilliant piece of work by his youngest brother, Thomas John, who read a paper on it in Dublin in 1851 to a meeting of the Institution of Civil Engineers presided over by the commissioner. The system was fifty years ahead of its time, according to eminent authorities a century later.

In retrospect, it seems a great pity that two extremely talented Irishmen, Rosse and Mulvany, both of whom were autodidactic engineers with significant achievements to their credit, did not meet in more cordial and happier circumstances. Had their unfortunate confrontation in the halls of Westminster (where they were polite but bitter protagonists) not taken place, who knows what a meeting of their minds might have brought forth for their own benefit and for that of their country?

Today, the Rosse Castle demesne in Birr, Co. Offaly, has one of the finest collections of exotic and rare plants in Western Europe. Its magnolias are the first to bloom in the Irish springtime and the re-constructed telescope is on view to the public.

8

Mulvany Resigns on Pension

Immediately following the issuing of the select committee's report, it would appear that Mulvany seriously considered retirement. He felt that he had become the scapegoat even though it had proved extremely difficult for the committee to brand him with incompetence, or worse.

Later in the same year, 1852, the Whig Party, under Lord Derby, came into power. One of its first acts was to drastically reduce the size of the civil service and other statutory bodies throughout Ireland and the British Isles. A Superannuation Act was introduced to induce longer serving staff to take early retirement.

Being a commissioner, Mulvany no longer had the status of a civil servant. His post was a political appointment. Yet, he was asked to remain on for a period of two years in order to supervise the completion of the drainage projects then in progress. He was given an increase in salary. But the vicissitudes of his work during and after the Famine years as well as the additional stress created by the enquiry had taken its toll on his health.

In 1854, he decided to retire from the Board of Works after 19 years' service. He had earned a good pension. As well as being a member of the Institution of Civil Engineers in Ireland, William Thomas was also a member of the Royal Irish Academy and the Geological and Zoological Society of Ireland.

In one sense, Mulvany ought to have been grateful to Lord Rosse for his actions for he had been placed once again at a crossroads in life. He had come to the end of a brilliant career at the comparatively early age of 48. Now fate would once more take a hand in his destiny.

He moved to London with the aim of seeking a change of air and indulged in outdoor sports in the hope of recovering his fitness and health. He had ample opportunity now to observe at close quarters some of the fruits of the Industrial Revolution that had virtually bypassed his native land. Brunell, Watt, Stephenson, and many other pioneers had seen their innovations and ideas proven in practice and exploited on a grand scale both at home and abroad. James Watt's son had piloted the first steam boat up the Rhine to Cologne and Stephenson's locomotive drew the first train from Nürnberg to Fürth in 1835.

Mulvany could see the infrastructure of Britain expanding to meet the demands of industrial and commercial development and could scarcely avoid comparing this with the conditions he had recently experienced at home. He was aware of the development of Britain's canal system, especially the Manchester Ship Canal which had taken a mere four years to build and had given the city a waterborne connection to the whole world. The impact of this project remained with him for many years.

During the first 13 years of the railway era a mere 123 miles of track were laid in Ireland, while in Belgium, with only half the population, over 347 miles were laid in the first eight years. When casting his mind back over his quarter of a century with the Board of Works and the Ordnance Survey, disappointments and frustrations had not dented his innovative and pioneering spirit.

In his last year in Dublin he had made the acquaintance of an Irishman who had been born in Slane, Co. Meath, and brought up in Brussels. In London, he again met this man, Michael Corr van der Maeren. Corr's father had been a furniture manufacturer in Bride's Alley, Dublin, and had been active in the 1798 rebellion. In 1802, he was about to be arrested by the police when he fled the country with his wife, leaving behind their two-week-old son, Michael.

The family was reunited again after the lifting of the blockade at the end of the Napoleonic War. Michael was then thirteen years of age. He went to school in Brussels and later joined the Belgian army, becoming an officer. Two other brothers also joined the Belgian or Netherlands forces and fought for the independence of those countries in 1830.

Upon leaving the army, he became a successful businessman and campaigned for the 'penny post'. He met and married a Flemish girl, the daughter of a prominent newspaper proprietor.

Michael Corr van der Maeren

As was the custom of the day, he added his wife's family name to his own and was then known as Michael Corr van der Maeren. He was a follower and close friend of Richard Cobden in England, one of the earliest champions of free trade. Corr van der Maeren founded the Société d'Économie Belge with the aim of abolishing customs posts between European countries.

At this time, entrepreneurs and investors in England, the Netherlands and Belgium began to make investments in the Prussian coal-fields that were undeveloped and under-capitalised. In fact, most of the capital for these mines was coming from outside the country. Corr van der Maeren had taken an interest in a small 'Mutung' or claim near Gelsenkirchen in the Rhineland. A common problem with the small mining operations along the Emscher River was the ingress of ground water.

When they met in London, Corr van der Maeren discussed this problem with Mulvany. Apparently, he was aware of the latter's reputation as a drainage engineer. No doubt, Mulvany apprised him of his experiments with screw pumps in the past. Some of these pumps had been employed in the construction of the canal between Tralee and Blennerhasset. All over the Rhineland, apparently, the presence of ground water close to the surface stultified any serious development, there being little knowledge or mechanical means to de-water the shafts. Corr van der Maeren had little difficulty in persuading Mulvany to make a brief visit to Gelsenkirchen to see the problem for himself.

In 1854, the Ruhrgebiet, as it is known today, was nothing like the present pulsating industrial area. At that time, the population of all the Prussian states was about 30 million. Vast areas of the Rhineland and Westphalia were covered in woods and forests. Towns were connected by untarred roads. Gelsenkirchen, with a population of just over 200, was a village set among trees. Düsseldorf, the largest town in the region, had a population of 30,000. Most industries were small, family-owned businesses employing less than 50 workers and production-line systems were still unheard of.

As in other economically developed countries, industrialisation brought a movement of people from the country to the cities. Living conditions in the towns were often catastrophic. As late as 1867 in Berlin, it was estimated that an average of 6–7 persons lived in one room. Single workers often rented half a bed. The best-paid workers were in the machine-building sector with an income of 13 thaler per week, while printers were paid 6–7 thalers and textile workers were close to existence level at 1–3 thaler per week. Every seventh building worker died in an accident, every third died of tuberculosis and more than two-thirds of all weavers died of the same disease. (*Deutsche Geschichte in Daten*, Jochen Schmidt-Liebich, dtv, München, 1981.)

The operating coal pits were very primitively equipped. Work down the shafts was dangerous and, as in England, both women and children were employed digging out and moving coal underground. Working conditions were extremely bad and a 13 to 17 hour shift was the norm. In all, there was a marked contrast between these living conditions and the surge of industrial progress then evident all over Britain. Twenty-five years later Mulvany tried to recall his first impressions:

> I could see what tremendous natural resources could be set in motion in order to fully exploit the beginning of industrial development in the Rhineland and Westphalia. I was convinced that these provinces in every regard possessed a wonderful richness. Upon my first short visit at the Regional Mining Council offices I saw the geological charts and immediately perceived what magnificent treasures were underneath the ground. I saw how lacking your railways were, how incomplete your canals and transport facilities were, and said at the time 'these people do not appreciate what they have got here'.

These first impressions triggered off in Mulvany's mind a new, and possibly latent, entrepreneurial spirit. He was excited by the opportunities awaiting exploitation. Up to then he probably knew very little about Europe in general and Prussia in particular and, Corr van der Maeren, with his knowledge of the Flemish language, was able to act as interpreter at these initial meetings.

Mulvany had lived and worked on the banks of a long and, in places, wide river. Then, as he stood on the banks of Europe's greatest river, the Rhine, he could observe that it was being used to transport goods over great distances from the North Sea up to Cologne, Mannheim and Heidelberg, despite the fact that the river was not yet regulated and the presence of numerous customs posts of the countries through which it flowed.

Around 1830, it was not believed that there were any valuable coal deposits along the Emscher River valley which marks the northern border of the present Ruhrgebiet. The seams were thought to be much further south. It was largely left to individual businessmen and speculators with financial resources, including non-nationals, to invest in trial borings, a difficult task which might take several days for each bore hole. Franz Haniel, a businessman whose mercantile dynasty still flourishes today, and who became a close friend of Mulvany, caused a sensation in 1847 when he found coal where none was thought to exist at a depth of only 47 metres in the Emscher Valley. By 1855, there were 150 applications to prospect for coal between Düsseldorf and Duisburg. Many of the seams were quite close to the surface but were only a few metres thick. Yet the coal was of a high quality.

Mulvany decided that his future career would be tied to developments in this region. The bad memories of his last two years in arterial drainage in Ireland began to fade and his mind was full of ideas of how to exploit the opportunities which were now open to him, albeit in a fully new and strange environment, among different people and with a different language. He returned to Dublin.

9

Raising Venture Capital in Ireland

In all probability, Mulvany had very little private means at his disposal, apart from his pension. More importantly, he had no experience of mining coal. Yet, he was determined to become involved in exploiting the claim in which Corr van der Maeren had invested near Gelsenkirchen. He met with James Perry, a brewer from Rathdowney, who was a friend of Corr's. Later he met Perry's brother, William, from Obelisk Park in Dublin. Mulvany also contacted Joseph Malcolmson, a shipowner, of Mayfield, and his brothers, William and David Malcolmson, of Portlaw, Co. Waterford. They were impressed by what Mulvany told them about his Prussian visit and agreed to invest money in developing the mine. A company was set up and the shareholding divided according to the size of investments. Mulvany took a minority shareholding but was largely responsible for setting up and managing the company.

Mulvany's next move was a visit to some English coal-fields, particularly those in Durham and Northumberland. He looked closely at the methods and equipment being used there. Most of the coal seams in England were quite deep, requiring the use of lifts and mechanical handling as well as efficient ventilation systems. These shafts also had mechanical steam-driven pumping systems to maintain safe water levels. He soon realised that the systems he had seen near Gelsenkirchen were makeshift by comparison.

At Apedale in Staffordshire, there were workings at 2,145 feet below the surface. Better handling of coal, he observed, led to higher output. But it was in Durham that he saw the most advanced technology. Here the system of sinking shafts and propping ceilings at the coalface promised the greatest efficiency and safety. Durham introduced the steel shuttering system, whereby prefabricated sections of concave sheeting attached by bolts to forged circular T-bars offered enormous savings in assembly time and made it much easier to keep seepage of ground water at bay. It was called the 'Tubing System'. The principle is still in use today, particularly in the construction of tunnels.

Mulvany was most impressed with this technology and resolved to use it in Westphalia. Bochum Museum has a section of this 'tubing' on permanent exhibition as well as the original system of wickerwork lining of the vertical shafts. In the Rhineland it was known as 'Tübbing'.

There can be little doubt about Mulvany's courage at this juncture. Although he had the able assistance of Corr van der Maeren, he knew very little about the legal and social systems in Prussia and, of course, he neither understood nor spoke the language. He had only a little knowledge of mining and marketing coal but that did not stop him. His career from the time he was nineteen years old had been among government officials at various ranks and his activities were governed by age-old rules and regulations in a distinctly hierarchical system. Personal enterprise was circumscribed and had its risks as well as its rewards. Now he was setting out on a path he would have to carve out himself without reference to precedents and would become the only Irish entrepreneur of the nineteenth century to set himself up in this part of the continent of Europe.

Only in the coal industry were non-nationals allowed to establish a 'Gewerk' or company in Prussia and hold all of the issued capital. The shares in mining were called 'kuxen' and a company was formed with 128 kuxen. Kuxe derives from the Czech and means 'part'. This company form, however, did not have the advantage for shareholders of limited liability which, though common in Britain, was only introduced in Prussian joint stock companies later.

The 'Mutungen' or claims were subject to a peculiar legal definition or category. The underground seams were not the property of the landowner, neither were they the property of the state, nor the 'Grafschaft' (county), but were, in legal terms, *nullius res*. Control and 'Mutungen' of potentially successful borings were registered at the Oberbergamt, the regional mining office, and could be traded freely. To distinguish mines or claims from each other owners registered distinctive titles and some very curious titles were created. The risk factor in coal-mining was, perhaps, best represented by names such as 'Glück' (luck), while it later became fashionable to choose names of well-known people or relatives, particularly female relatives of the owners. Mulvany decided upon a name, Hibernia, that was revealed on the next St Patrick's Day.

The coal in this region generally was of a very high quality and not very far below the surface in many cases. The land appears to have been sold at a comparatively low cost and, therefore, was attracting foreign speculators as there were no limitations on foreign investment in the country, nor on the percentage of shares a foreigner might hold in a company.

From his first visit in the summer of 1854 until the spring of

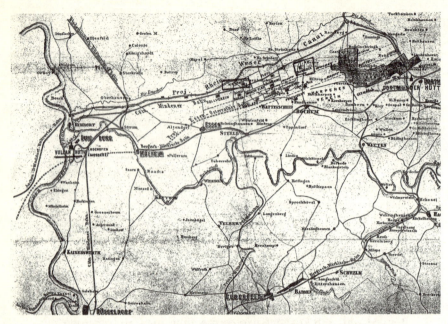

Ruhrgebiet, around 1870, showing Hibernia, Shamrock and Castrop mines and the Vulkan Blast furnaces

James Perry and Joseph Malcolmson

1855, Mulvany worked at organising the projected investment. On his next visit, he inspected a number of potential areas and established a good rapport with the Oberbergamt in Dortmund where he met Krug von Nidda, then head of the Prussian Mining Office. He established a close and enduring friendship with von Nidda.

In November 1854, only a few months after Mulvany's initial foray into the Rhineland, Corr van der Maeren, acting on behalf of James Perry, Mulvany and himself, purchased additional shares in two small claims in the village of Gelsenkirchen (population then 200, now 290,000). These bore the names 'Christianglück' and 'Ludwigsglück'. The owners of these claims were Ludwig von Ovens, a wealthy pensioner, and Samuel Ryland Phipson, a financial broker in Brussels. The price paid was 4,551 thalers and 2,275 thalers, respectively. Twenty-five years later, these claims were valued at 500,000 marks, a substantial appreciation in value. The four partners divided the shares as follows: 44 kuxen for von Ovens with the remainder divided equally between Corr van der Maeren, James Perry and Mulvany.

In Dublin, Mulvany contacted other friends and acquaintances to try to interest them in making an investment in these coal-mines. He must have had only a vague idea of the capital requirement for the exploitation due to his lack of experience in the industry. Yet, he was able to persuade a number of wealthy Irish merchants to participate in a venture capital project in a foreign country. The new investors were two members of the Perry family, James Perry jun., and William James Perry of Obelisk Park, Dublin, and the brothers Joseph, William and David Malcolmson, manufacturers and shipowners, of Portlaw.

In hindsight, it is curious that during a period when Ireland, as a country, was extremely poor with a population living at a bare existence level, there should be any speculative capital available for investment. Yet, Robert Kane wrote in 1845 that £2 million yearly were being transferred from Ireland to England for the purchase of government bonds and the value of shipping shares belonging to investors in Dublin was only exceeded by those in London and was greater than those in Bristol, Hull, and Liverpool together. (*The Industrial Resources of Ireland*, 1845, p. 409).

Shortly afterwards the shareholders travelled to Gelsenkirchen on a site inspection. They met afterwards in the Breidenbacher Hof, then and still one of Düsseldorf's leading hotels. Von Ovens' kuxen were acquired as well as those of Phipson and the shareholding was restructured as follows:

Joseph Malcolmson	40
William Malcolmson	8
William Thomas Mulvany	16
Michael Corr van der Maeren	16
David Malcolmson	8
James Perry, junior	8
James Perry, senior	<u>32</u>
Total	128 kuxen

From this point on the ownership of the claims to the two as yet unexcavated coal-fields were totally in Irish hands. The investors agreed that the responsibility for the entire project, including technical management and development of the mines as well as the marketing and sale of the coal, would be in Mulvany's hands. He was given the title of 'Representative' with a fixed salary of £500 as well as a commission of 5% on net profits. All travel costs and expenditure on behalf of the company would be reimbursed. In the event of his death, his relatives should receive half of this sum for a period of seven years. This financial arrangement put Mulvany in very good circumstances, especially in the successful years that followed. He appears to have been given a very free hand. The shareholders were older and unlikely to have spent much time in Prussia. Board meetings were held in Düsseldorf, London and Dublin in the years that followed.

The Malcolmson family of Co. Waterford, who were Quakers, held nearly half of the share capital in the Hibernia and later in the Shamrock mines in Herne. The industrial revolution in Britain had spawned many venture capital enterprises in the early 1800s. The Malcolmsons had come from Scotland and originally were weavers. They settled in Lurgan in the north of Ireland and were prominent in the linen trade. Typical for Quakers, they had large families, in this instance eleven children. Two young sons, John and David, were sent to Clonmel to learn the corn-milling business and this enterprise prospered and expanded to Portlaw and Carrick-on-Suir. By 1850, the company employed 1,800 workers and Portlaw became a modern 'factory town'.

In 1825 David, then sixty years of age, opened a cotton mill in Portlaw, which also prospered. Raw cotton was imported from America. David died in 1844 at 79 years of age. By this time, the family was involved in and were shareholders in railways, shipping lines (P&O), fisheries as well as milling. As an extension of their interest in shipping the family set up the Neptune Iron Works in Waterford in 1843, primarily, at first, to repair vessels. Soon a paddle-steamer, the SS *Neptune*, was the first ship off the stocks. From then onwards the shipyard built a variety of ships, 40 in all, before it closed in 1882. Many of these vessels were large for their time, some being of 4,000 tons displacement. In the shipyard, skilled men received 27 shillings per week and worked 10 hours a day, six days a week. Unskilled workers received a third of this rate. In the Clonmel corn mills workers received one pound sterling per week for an 11-hour day.

The Malcolmsons had amassed considerable wealth and despite the virtual collapse of the cotton trade due to lack of supplies during the American Civil War (1861–1865), their other operations expanded. It is not surprising, therefore, that Mulvany's approach to them seeking participation in financing the mines in the Ruhr in 1854–55 met with an immediate response. The brothers Joseph and William Malcolmson lived in large residences, one in Dunmore East (now the Haven Hotel), three in Portlaw (Clodagh, Elva and Woodlock) and one in Clonmel (Minella) and had money to invest.

William Malcolmson is said to have invested unwisely, several of his projects having failed. The family's London bankers, Overend and Gurney, known for their many Quaker clients, went bankrupt in 1877 with losses in the region of thirteen million pounds, much of this belonging to the Waterford family. That same year the family business was declared bankrupt and the shipyard closed down finally in 1882, a sad end to the fortunes of this remarkable and enterprising clan of Irish merchant princes.

Fred Malcolmson

George Malcolmson

Henry Perry

10

Mulvany Family Moves to Düsseldorf

In 1851, the Prussian government passed a law which allowed mining companies a substantial degree of private ownership and autonomy without the previous authoritarian interference of government-appointed officials. This helped to develop private enterprise in industrial sectors as well as new banking institutions. As a result of this progress, mainly in the urban areas, there was a significant population growth in the Ruhr cities of Düsseldorf, Duisburg, Essen and Dortmund, though generally the region was still dominated by agriculture and forestry. In Prussia in 1815, the population was 28 million. By 1870, it had grown to 40 million. The rail network expanded from 549 km in 1840 to 6,044 km in 1850 and 19,579 km in 1870.

A new life in a foreign country with a different language began for Mulvany. In the autumn of 1855, when the harvest had been saved several additional borings were sunk in the fields around Gelsenkirchen and Mulvany acquired the rights to these. He established good relations with the officers of the Oberbergamt in Dortmund and received much support from them. Not only was the language barrier an impediment but also there were obvious differences in character to be found in the people of the provinces. The Rhineland, Westphalia, Hesse, Baden, Württemberg, Bavaria, and the other northern and eastern provinces, were states with independent autonomies which were only brought together later under Bismarck.

Mulvany could discern distinct differences in the characters of Rhinelanders and Westphalians. The Westphalians were dour, conservative farming folk, not given to changing their lifestyle, but hard-working and skilful in the cultivation of the land. Rhinelanders were more enterprising, quick to develop their industrial potential and more open to foreign business and culture.

Before the winter of 1855, Mulvany moved his family to Düsseldorf. He rented an apartment in the fashionable Karlstor district, in Poststrasse, close to the present parliament buildings. Robert and Clara Schumann lived nearby, and the young Johannes Brahms was a family friend and a great admirer of Clara.

Mulvany must have been a welcome representative of British viewpoints on current affairs for Krug von Nidda, the influential head of the Dortmund Mining Council Office. He could exchange his own first-hand high-level experience of the workings of the British civil service and government agencies and learn of the attitudes and practices obtaining in Westphalia at that time. Gradually he became known in business circles and was invited to comment and advise on current developments as he, the informed stranger, saw them.

Mulvany's task was not easy. Well grounded as he was in the British administrative system he had to adjust to an entrenched and very bureaucratic Prussian system. There was less freedom of political expression than at home. Civil administrators had very wide powers and innovators were often barely tolerated rather than encouraged. One of the first things that struck Mulvany was the poor progress in the development of the infrastructure, particularly the railways. The main line of the day, the Köln-Minden Railway virtually by-passed the Ruhr region and the existing mines had no proper railheads.

Mulvany quickly made many friends, some of them prominent and influential, including Dr Friedrich Hammacher, a leading Liberal politician, and Franz and Hugo Haniel, founders of a shipbuilding and transport dynasty which still flourishes today. In Prussian eyes, Mulvanny seemed proud of his Irish background but had the manners and poise of what they considered the perfect Englishman. He had extensive knowledge to impart on the progress of industrial enterprises in Ireland and Britain which was readily acknowledged to be way ahead of the Prussian status. His criticism of the railways and canals was accepted and appreciated as it came from an expert.

In Prussia, there was admiration and envy for British industrial achievements. Stephenson's *Adler* was the first steam locomotive to open the stretch between Nürnberg and Fürth in 1835. Humphrey Davey's invention of the safety lamp was a great improvement in safety for mining. Faraday, the blacksmith's son from Southwark, was discovering the principles of electricity leading to the invention of the electric motor, the generator and radio signals. The engineer Brassey was building railways in Canada, Australia, South America and in India. The Great Exhibition of London in 1851 attracted 13,000 exhibitors and six million visitors from home and abroad. At the time, 60% of world shipping sailed under the British flag and Britain's cotton industry was the biggest in the world.

The Crimean War (1854–56) engaged Britain in the doubtful game of power politics for obscure and disputed reasons. It cost fifty million pounds and 22,000 British, 70,000 French and 75,000 Russian lives. The London financial houses had no compunction in floating a Russian loan at the same time.

The Prussian states were engrossed in internecine rivalries which inhibited development and utilisation of natural resources on a wide and rationalised scale. Family-owned businesses dominated the economy. At this time Krupp, already renowned for its steel production, was employing 500 workers. By contrast, Middlesborough in 1850 was just a village, but by 1870 was a large urban community supplying one-third of Britain's output of pig iron. This expansion was helped by progressive banking and financial services, something still lacking in Prussia.

Mulvany found himself propagating the English work ethos to an interested and alert business community. An official ceremony was held in Gelsenkirchen by the Irish investors on 17 March, St Patrick's Day, 1856, and local dignitaries attended. The commencement of work on the new mine was celebrated by turning the first sod and the mine was given the name 'Hibernia'. A reception was held afterwards in the restaurant of the newly-built railway station which now had a link to the Köln-Minden line.

The other shareholders, the Malcolmsons and the Perrys particularly, observed how well Mulvany was already integrated into the local commercial life and were assured of his capacity to get things done without unnecessary delay. How much capital they invested is not recorded although the minutes of early meetings are archived in Bochum's Museum. Minutes were written up in English and German.

Gelsenkirchen was unique at that time in having a new rail link. Most of the existing mines had to rely on horse-drawn transport for getting the coal to their outlets or nearest canal. Mulvany realised that, if he were to succeed, he must do things very differently from what then obtained in Westphalia. One of his first steps was to recruit a very experienced mining engineer, Louis C. König, to assist him. Most existing pits were small with very little mechanical equipment. Major problems were the extraction of the ground water and ventilation of shafts. But the seams were not very deep by comparison with those in England, Scotland and Wales and this meant less time and less cost would be required in sinking shafts. He was determined to get the necessary technology from England and went, with König, on an extended visit to the coal-fields in Britain. Both were able to observe at close hand many developments which had made the British mines so viable.

One of the main achievements had been the virtual integration of the railways and the coal-mines so that every colliery had a railhead. Furthermore, the cost of moving coal from the pit-head to the main outlets such as the cities and ports was subsidised, thus positively influencing the cost to the customer, especially the blast furnaces. Although the shafts in Britain were in the main much deeper than in Westphalia, steam-driven equipment was being utilised for the internal transport of coal, for the ventilation systems and for the extraction of water.

Mulvany noted all these methods carefully and went a step further. He and König recruited a number of skilled miners in Durham and Northumberland and took them and their families to Gelsenkirchen. Mulvany purchased land and built single-storey terraced houses for the miners and their families in what today is Schwanstrasse, Neustadt. The district later became known as Balaclava, after the famous battle in the Crimean War. The inventor of the 'Tübbing' system as it was called, William Coulson, an engineer, was engaged to supervise the transfer. Most of these English miners remained in Gelsenkirchen all their lives. The last one, George Laverick, died there in 1913.

Over succeeding years 300 English and Irish workers were brought to Gelsenkirchen. From the beginning, Mulvany instituted a regular religious Sunday service and established a school to teach the thirty children living there. English family names such as Patterson, Simpson, Dreyden and Laverick survived in Gelsenkirchen for generations afterwards. A contemporary account reported that the English miners got on well with their German neighbours and brought welcome custom to local businesses. Their living standard was better than that of their neighbours. Their diet consisted of white bread,

William Coulson with Durham miners

Housing for miners built by Mulvany

baked daily by their wives, meat, butter and cheese. At that time, the German diet was mainly potatoes, vegetables and fat bacon. The English housewives eagerly bought up the varieties of mushrooms growing in Gelsenkirchen's meadows.

The Durham miners were fond of athletics and introduced football, a pastime soon taken up by their neighbours. Disputes, it was noted, were rarely settled with the knife or revolver, but rather with rolled-up sleeves and fisticuffs in the street. Such bouts were usually observed by the wives often smoking clay pipes. In the late summer, lawn tennis tournaments were held with parties and dancing. English miners received ten marks per shift while their German colleagues received only two marks.

When the First World War broke out in 1914 the English families then living in Gelsenkirchen and Herne were given the option of surrendering their British citizenship, which they still held, and becoming naturalised German citizens or returning to England. Some returned, others remained. In 1992, I met and interviewed a grandson of a miner from Durham with the family name Dreyden or Dryden with a kinship to John Dryden, the poet. Under British law, grandchildren of British citizens could claim the use of British passports and Thomas Robert Mulvany had signed a passport for Dryden's grandfather in his capacity of Consul General in Düsseldorf at

Haus Thionville on Kaiserswerther Strasse. This passport enabled Mr Dryden to represent a large German concern in India in 1945–46 when German citizens were not allowed into the British Commonwealth. He was born and lived in his youth in Shamrockstrasse, Herne, and used to have a weekly bath in the mine's facilities.

When a number of Irish workers were recruited, Mulvany arranged for a Catholic chaplain, Father Sebastiani, to attend to their spiritual needs. Later, when Fr Sebastiani retired, these workers presented him with a chalice and an address of thanks which they all signed. This document was one of the few items to survive the bombing of the Second World War (see Appendix II).

William Coulson, Inventor of 'Tübbing' system

Wappen der Stadt Herne

Coat of arms of Herne, 1900–1975

11

Modern Technical Systems and Equipment

Visitors to the Mining Museum in Bochum today can see models of the various methods of sinking shafts, including a segment of the 'Tübbing' system.

The new systems introduced by Mulvany had a profound effect generally on mine construction. These and other innovations were quickly emulated and became standard practice in other mines in the region. He also introduced a double-shaft system. This not only improved mass-production potential but also made for greater safety underground as the second shaft could be used for circulating 'Wetter' (air). An end effect was the production of cleaner and better quality coal. A degree of rationalisation was achieved through the installation of large winches with steel hawsers to transport wagons underground.

Fifteen months after its foundation the first coal was taken out of the 'Hibernia' mine from a level of 111.6 metres. The seam was virtually on a horizontal level, a most important advantage. By the following summer, 200 workers were producing 200 tons of good quality coal per shift. By 1858, Hibernia's coal production was at the level of 18,000 tons per annum and by 1872, it rose to 148,000 tons. At that stage the workforce numbered 852 persons. It continued production until 1926 and after 67 years in operation, a total of 18.4 million tons of coal was won from the earth.

When Mulvany moved his family to Düsseldorf, he also took his widowed mother as his father had died in 1845 in Dublin. He induced his younger brother, Thomas John, who also had become a commissioner in the Board of Works, to resign his position, forfeit a pension, and join the company as technical director of Hibernia. Mulvany's son, Thomas Robert, was given a practical apprenticeship down the mines at 16 years of age.

In 1857, in the Ruhrgebiet there were 151 mines in operation, many of them small ventures. In all, 12,503 workers were employed or an average of 83 per mine.

From the start, Hibernia was successful. It was efficient thanks to the new technology that had been introduced and found a ready outlet for its good quality coal. Mulvany was by then *au fait* with the general state of the mining industry in the region and was consulted by the Dortmund Mining Office on improving and rationalising operations in other mines. The Hibernia mine set standards which were followed by the industry as a whole.

His brother Thomas John had established a reputation in the Board of Works which rivalled that of his elder brother, especially in the use of pumps to drain canals and rivers. His work on the screw pump was well known: this was probably an early form of the impeller principle. For mines with water problems, and there were plenty in the Ruhr area, this kind of equipment was an absolute necessity.

Thomas John took over responsibility for technical management and William Thomas concentrated on marketing as well as seeking out new opportunities. He wanted to expand and on 23 October 1856, he wrote to the Bochum Regional Mining Office indicating that he had purchased two new claims, Merkania 1 and Merkania 2, which he wished to amalgamate under the name 'Shamrock'. He also requested approval to sink the first shaft which was close to the town of Herne. It then had a population of about 1,400.

Official approval for the new Shamrock mine was given within the record period of eight days but it was decided to wait until the following February to commence actual work. A report issued in April 1857 stated:

> At the Shamrock Mine which is ten minutes west of Herne on a plot of ground purchased by the company, about 56 morgen (26 hectares), the sinking of a shaft was commenced during the month of March and a total of 31 feet was sunk with a diameter of 21 feet 9 inches. As this clay strata was sufficiently solid the lining was begun with brick and mortar 31 feet high and a wall thickness of 27 inches.

It is interesting to note the use of feet and inches in this report. The measurements in use at the time were lachters (2.092m) and Prussian inches (2.615 cm).

The Bochum Regional Mining Office took a keen interest in the progress of the work not only to ensure that adequate safety measures were being taken but also to see the new technology from England which Mulvany was introducing. While the 'Tübbing' method did not entirely replace brickwork, it made a major contribution towards safety and water control.

One of Thomas John's first tasks was the planning and securing permission for the building of provisional workers' living accommodation as well as a small effluent canal, a materials' store, a smithy,

The Shamrock mine in Herne

stables for horses and a brick oven. Later plans were submitted for six houses for skilled employees and their families from England. Afterwards additional land was purchased and, most importantly, a railhead was built which gave access to the main line Cologne-Minden Railway.

The Shamrock mine became the main economic pillar of Herne and its environs over the following century. In 1932 there were 3,500 miners employed producing coal at an annual rate of 715,000 tons. During the Second World War, the installations suffered severe damage through bombing raids but by 1950, they were back in business and employing 2,300 workers.

Mulvany extended the Shamrock activity to include the production of coke for the steel furnaces. A large number of beehive coke ovens were set up for this purpose. It was an early attempt at achieving vertical integration in the exploitation of a natural resource.

However, the development of the coal industry did not happen without opposition. The local, mostly farming, population noticed the pace with which these plans and works were conducted. Inevitably, there was a reaction. Protests were made claiming potential damage to the landscape and to wells and ground water. Mulvany had to reassure the protesters that care would be taken not to interfere with water resources in the Herne district. They also complained about the effect on the environment and, indeed, on the poorly-made roads in their districts. The railways, too, with their noise and smoking locomotives, were the subject of complaint.

Apart from the Hibernia mine in Gelsenkirchen and the Shamrock project, some 150 mine shafts were already operational in the Emscher Valley, though most of these were very small units with little or no sophisticated equipment. Still, they gave employment to 12,503 workers with an average output of 607 tons per man per year. In addition, there were 20 coke producers with 401 ovens.

The Mining Office in Bochum maintained close contact with the new Shamrock project. All activities, especially the sinking of the first vertical shaft, were required to receive official sanction before the commencement of work. In addition, the company had to submit regular progress reports. The speed with which Mulvany received approval, a matter of days, suggests that his submission was quite detailed and convincing or that he already had an inside track among the officials. Perhaps a little of both was the case. Seen from the viewpoint of the Mining Office the Hibernia and Shamrock projects with their ample financial funding from abroad were very welcome in this undeveloped region especially because of the new technology and equipment which had been proven in the coal-fields of Northumberland and Durham.

In April 1857, the first commercially usable coal was taken out from a depth of about 271 metres. Using one and a quarter inch wire hawser with a hemp core, a load of about 700 kilos could be hauled to the surface in two bogeys. Mining officials kept in close touch with developments and made frequent visits to the works to inspect and observe that safety measures were being installed and maintained. By August 1860, the office drew up a set of by-laws and the names of staff members responsible for individual departments were noted. Responsibility for mechanical operations rested in the person of G. Laverick and Wm. Lattimore; I. Griffith was in charge of lifts and James Graham was responsible for the Übertage (surface) operations. It is interesting to note the use of Übertage and Untertage to denote surface and underground (literally, above day and below day).

In 1861, the first problems with the workforce arose. A number, not all, went on strike without the necessary fourteen days' notice being given to the management. Mulvany was upset and wrote to the Bürgermeister complaining about this lightning strike and the efforts of some militant workers to coerce others to come out with them. He requested assistance from the police in maintaining law and order, especially at shift change times, normally at 4 a.m., 12 noon and evenings at 8 o'clock. It is possible that he wrote his memorandum on workers' rights and obligations at this time (see Appendix I).

Around this time, the use of Davey's safety lamp became mandatory and it is recorded that 250 of these lamps were available for 160 to 170 miners per shift. T. J. Mulvany advised the Mining Office that a second pit was planned to be called Shamrock II with a depth of 198 metres and a circumference of 10 feet. The same 'Tübbing' system and brickwork would be used as in Hibernia. A section of this plating has been preserved and may be seen in the Bochum Mining Museum.

Unlike the Hibernia operation, the Shamrock mines had very little water seepage and the first coal was taken out within 12 months. In 1858, Shamrock produced 21,928 tons of coal with 200 workers and by 1872 was producing 190,000 tons with 952 workers.

Over a period of about twelve years the two mines, Hibernia and Shamrock, continued to operate successfully even when other sections of the industry were having ups and down. Indeed, a feature of the history of the coal industry is the see-saw trend in results over very many decades right up to the present day. No doubt, the Irish venture had the edge on its rivals because of the technology installed initially. Two major impediments facing the Prussian coal industry were the lack of rail connections at the pitheads and the fact that British coal was being marketed in Prussia at lower prices than the local product. The fact that British coal was cheaper in northern Prussia and even in Berlin gave Mulvany much food for thought, especially as he had been a close supporter of his friend, Corr van der Maeren, who championed the cause of free trade. Mulvany changed his mind on this issue and pressed for measures to introduce import tariffs on coal coming from England.

Mulvany had become a man of means and had an imposing villa amidst a sylvan park in the Düsseldorf suburb of Pempelfort. His brother lived in a substantial residence on the Shamrock site in Herne. The elder Mulvany had become an influential figure in the Rhineland and Westphalia and he published and distributed a number of memoranda on practical issues. Some of the original Irish investors were getting old and the Malcolmsons suffered the ignominy of bankruptcy at home. At some stage, the Malcolmsons found fault with the way the company's financial affairs were being conducted and there was a confrontation at board meetings. The only evidence of the internal dispute is a press report which mentioned the granting by the city fathers of Gelsenkirchen of the Freedom of the

City to W. T. Mulvany in gratefulness for what he had contributed to that city's economic development.

The mines continued to operate until October 1967, when a general recession again hit the industry. Over the years from 1857 until 1967, Shamrock produced a total of 62.3 million tons of coal. The downward trend in mining has continued. In the 1970s, about 130,000 workers were employed in mining in Germany and today that number has fallen to about 40,000. By 2005, this figure will fall to approximately 25,000 with possibly only three or four mines operating.

Coal-mining cannot be discussed without mention of the many tragedies that beset this industry over the centuries. Hibernia, Shamrock and later the Erin mines had their share of mining disasters. On 10 March 1906, in Courrières, northern France, one of the worst disasters in European mining history occurred. An explosion cut off 1,539 miners underground with very little hope of being rescued. The French management, aware of the good safety record of Hibernia, sent an urgent appeal for assistance. A twenty-man team of trained rescue workers were sent to France. They succeeded in rescuing 14 of those trapped but, despite weeks of efforts, the remainder were brought out dead. G. A. Mayer, Hibernia's manager, was awarded the Legion of Honour and a band of friendship developed between French and German miners afterwards. A street leading to the site of the Shamrock mine in Herne is named Courrieresstrasse.

F. W. Pabst, the famous film director, made a film on the subject, *Kameradschaft* in 1932. It was a German-French co-production and was aimed at reconciling relations between the two countries after the First World War. Most of the scenes in the film were shot in the Hibernia and Shamrock mines.

12

Technical and Commercial Management

Working conditions in the mines at this period in the nineteenth century were not much above the level of slavery. Reconstruction of the shafts and pits in a 1:1 scale may be seen at the Comprehensive Mining Museum in Bochum. This gives a very graphic impression of the physical effort and the psychological stress in the dark, confined, dusty and dangerous galleries with the ever-present fear of gas explosions. Fortunately, the early years of the two mines were without major accident and it was not until 1887 and 1891 that explosions occurred with the loss of 50 lives on each occasion.

The passages were often just wide enough for one person to creep through and headroom was a luxury. Hewers of coal had to work long hours on bended knees in this dust-filled atmosphere. Accidents and injuries were frequent. Young boys, barely into their teens, were employed in large numbers, mainly because they were better able to get through the shafts. As in England, women were employed to push or pull the trolleys or carts to the foot of the shaft for hoisting to the surface. The teenage boys, because of their size, were known as 'gnomes'. Later small ponies were introduced for this work.

A basic piecework system was operated, known as a 'Gedinge' – the norm set for the number of trolleys of coal hauled from the coalface. When this number fell below that set by the foreman or the load contained 'Berg' or earth from the edges of the seams, part of the wage was simply deducted. There were other sharp practices administered by strict disciplinarians and Mulvany, as one may deduce from his writings, put a high store on discipline. Perhaps his early years working under army engineers had left its mark.

Around 1850 the principle of conveyor belt production in manufacturing industries – separating component manufacture and assembly of finished products – began to establish itself. Up to then factories were more like centralised manual work centres, with few skilled operatives and large numbers of unskilled labour. The trend towards streamlined production with separate and repetitive work stations in over-crowded, badly-ventilated and unheated shops, long hours and minimal wages, gave rise to much agitation but the oversupply of labour gave employers the advantage. The break with the traditional manual crafts was accompanied by unrest and resentment among workers. Around this time, the move for more social justice in Prussia began to take root with socialists like Lassalle playing a leading role.

There was substantial variation in wages between the regions. Shifts of between 13 and 17 hours were common. Generally, miners earned better wages than their colleagues above ground and most of the unskilled workers were employed on a daily basis.

In the early part of the nineteenth century, many mines, small as they were, were under government control and regional mining offices such as those in Bochum and Essen were set up to augment the work of the main office in Dortmund. The function of these offices was to approve the establishment of the mines especially with regard to safety measures. These mines were privatised over a period but the mining inspectors monitored all operations underground.

A reform of the legislation in 1851 granted the miner and his dependents certain social benefits not then available to other workers. From early times, miners had enjoyed a modicum of social welfare but now with the establishment of the 'Knappschaften', or guilds, this was set out in more concrete terms. A social package to include illness benefit, hospital costs, funeral costs, and a widows' and orphans' fund was introduced and these measures set standards for all industrial workers. In this respect, the miners were better off than their colleagues in other countries.

The guilds, which operated these social security funds, were managed by committees elected on a 50:50 basis by the owners and the miners. It was the beginning of the doctrine, at first in matters of social affairs but later in management itself, of 'Mitbestimmung' or co-determination which in post-Second World War years became the mainspring of the Montanunion, the coal and steel industry alliance in Germany.

While Hibernia and Shamrock were producing good quality coal of different grades suitable for firing boilers and blast furnaces, magnates such as Krupp and Thyssen were expanding. The Irish-owned mines were earning good dividends in these early years with a net profit of 10% being achieved. This performance and more importantly, the efficiency of the mines with much innovative equipment, had a very positive impact on the industry generally. The towns of Gelsenkirchen and Herne began to grow rapidly as the spin-off effect of the successful mines became apparent.

A shareholders' meeting was held in Dublin on 26 September 1863, at which a rift among the shareholders became apparent. Mulvany found himself at odds with some of the other directors, notably William Malcolmson, who held a large proportion of the shares. Malcolmson questioned the manner of keeping the accounts and pressed for a reduction in Mulvany's emoluments in order to appoint a book-keeper. This was a great disappointment to Mulvany as he had borne most of the responsibility for the start-up and development of the project himself. There may have been grounds for criticising the financial control of the company in its initial years.

The Malcolmson family between them now held 64 out of the total 128 kuxen which put them in a dominant position. Mulvany was very reluctant to agree to the change sought in the management of the company and a sharp dispute took place. It was only through the intervention of Corr van der Maeren that the matter was finally resolved. Malcolmson had his way and a former bank manager, S. W. Perrot, was appointed accounts manager of Hibernia and Shamrock.

Some records of the Hibernia Company have survived and are archived in the Bochum Mining Museum, including the manuscript minutes of some board meetings. They are mainly concerned with the movement of shares within the original group of investors. A new shareholder was introduced – Patrick C. Roney, a railway director in London, took up 8 kuxen. At another stage the eight children of Marcus Goodbody, miller, were registered. These shares were transferred by one of the Perrys, who were relatives, and were held in trust until they reached 24 years of age. It was usual to make gifts of shares as wedding presents and Mulvany gave his daughter, Mary, one share when she married Wilhelm Hermann Seebohm, a mining engineer from Silesia and a member of the first Quaker family in Prussia.

A perusal of the dividend rates paid over the years reveals that after the initial very satisfactory period there was a downturn in results. There were several reasons for this, including growing competition, over-production and a series of economic crises, especially in the aftermath of the Franco-Prussian War (1870–1871).

A contributing factor was that the railways and the canals had not kept pace with the developments in mining. As a result, there was a major shortage of rolling stock to service the mines, resulting in the build-up of stocks of coal on the surface which could not be moved to customers. Mulvany addressed this problem in a memorandum entitled: 'Praktische Vorschläge zur Beseitigung der Transportnot' (Practical Suggestions for the Solution of the Transport Emergency).

From June 1858, the first pit of Hibernia was in operation and producing 200 tons per day. The table below illustrates the production and workforce employed between the years 1858 to 1872 during which time the mine was in Irish ownership:

Year	Production (tons)	Workforce	Year	Production (tons)	Workforce
1858	18,371	195	1866	120,568	685
1859	98,466	537	1867	141,990	726
1860	148,853	583	1868	176,651	822
1861	162,043	550	1869	188,800	815
1862	169,943	527	1870	168,270	722
1863	164,047	533	1871	165,450	828
1864	158,425	516	1872	148,210	852
1865	154,032	593			

Between 1860 and 1872 the following tonnage was produced in the Shamrock mine:

Year	Production (tons)	Workforce	Year	Production (tons)	Workforce
1858	---	162	1866	154,533	715
1859	---	154	1867	172,727	826
1860	21,428	210	1868	118,846	618
1861	98,023	430	1869	181,169	743
1862	139,604	550	1870	158,454	664
1863	144,431	614	1871	143,568	717
1864	157,251	585	1872	190,030	952
1865	172,259	637			

Herne   Zeche Shamrock I u. II.

A postcard from Herne, showing the two Shamrock mines

13

Mulvany Made First Freeman of Gelsenkirchen

On 28 August 1864, Mulvany became the first person to receive the freedom of the city of Gelsenkirchen. The *Essener Zeitung* reported:

> Today a deputation consisting of Herren Amtmann Gols, Mönting, Franke, Niewöhner, Raberschulte and Herbert, went to Düsseldorf to present the Freedom of our town, for which he has done very much, to Mr William Thomas Mulvany. The accompanying address was worded:
>
> 'About ten years ago you came to Gelsenkirchen in order with your talent to direct this company. You found Gelsenkirchen still in an uneconomic state, with bad roads, an unimportant station on the Köln-Minden Railway. With untiring effort you invested your remarkable energy into the responsibilities you assumed. You were an example of application and showed us what a strong will and clear understanding will achieve.
>
> 'Now Gelsenkirchen is an expanding town, its houses reflect affluence, and it has become an important station on the railway. The name of Gelsenkirchen is, through its coal, known in farthest lands, in foreign parts of the earth. You, honoured sir, have laid the foundation stone for all of this. Forgive us, therefore, when the thought of a total parting is painful. When we ask you to remain close to the affairs of our community in the future, and kindly accept the accompanying certificate as an indication of our recognition and high esteem. We ask you to keep us gladly in your thoughts and high esteem. We shall not forget the man of whom we can be proud and who has given honour to all our coal-mining.
>
> 'It is a pleasure to see how our community recognises the advantages brought by you to its industry and how it grants the man who laid the foundation stone of Gelsenkirchen's development the greatest honour a community can grant, that of Honorary Citizenship in grateful recognition.'

Despite political uncertainties in the mid-1860s, by 1868 the market for coal had stabilised and commenced to expand once again. Mulvany went to Berlin to try to obtain government support for the imposition of import tariffs for coal. He did not succeed but did obtain lower handling charges for coal on exportation. Together with his friend, Franz Haniel, founder of the transport dynasty, he visited many of the German ports and was dismayed to discover that not only were German-owned steamers calling at British ports for bunkers, because coal was cheaper there, but also units of the Kaiser's fleet had been following this example. A strong *démarche* by the two friends in the appropriate quarters in Berlin put an end to this practice.

The timing of the Irish investors' engagement was propitious. Between 1850 and 1860, the industry boomed. Economic development in various industrial sectors such as iron and steel, textiles, machine building as well as rolling stock placed an enormous demand on energy resources. Coal and coke production was vital in their expansion.

The boom did not last very long and in early 1871, a depression hit the coal and iron industry again. Many mines were forced to close and only the efficiency of operations saved Hibernia and Shamrock. Around this time, two of the founding shareholders, Joseph Malcolmson and James Perry, died, and in 1872 the remaining members decided to seek a purchaser. Mulvany, Frederick Malcolmson and William Cherry Robinson, who had joined the company, signed an agreement of sale to the Berliner Handelsgesellschaft and the C. Bleichröder-Berlin Bank of Hibernia and Shamrock for the sum of 5,786,000 thaler. The company was re-constituted under the name 'Hibernia und Shamrock Bergwerksgesellschaft zu Bochum'. Bleichröder was Otto von Bismarck's banker.

William Thomas Mulvany was invited to remain on the board as chairman for the remainder of his life and he and his brother, Thomas John, were given seats on the supervisory board. In 1873, a profit of 13% was achieved but by 1879 it had dropped to 3.3%. Again in 1880, the position improved and following modernisation of the plant it was again to the forefront in productivity.

Financial Results Gross Profits (presumably before tax):

Year	Shamrock Marks	Hibernia Marks	Total Marks
1873	804,889	864,300	1,669,289
1874	444,526	839,851	1,284,378
1875	160,538	330,680	491,218
1876	350,887	198,952	549,840
1877	334,692	329,785	654,478
1878	384,249	322,262	706,511
1879	469,697	337,725	807,423
1880	653,255	592,161	1,245,416
1881	419,546	526,784	946,330
1882	487,821	576,460	1,064,281
1883	661,046	694,604	1,355,651
1884	612,482	869,495	1,481,978
1885	800,974	681,140	1,482,114

Share coupon of Erin with the engraved portrait of Mulvany, still current before closure in 1983

14

The Prussian Mining and Iron Company

After the death of Joseph Malcolmson and James Perry, Mulvany got an opportunity to take over two bankrupt mines, Hansa and Zollern, at a cheap price. A blast furnace named Vulkan, in Duisburg on the Rhine, as well as iron ore deposits in the Westerwald, were included in the deal. He used his own capital and, with his brother, son, and Henry Bewley, Wilton Park, Dublin, as well as some of the Hibernia shareholders and directors of the Berlin Bank, purchased the assets from the liquidator. He registered the name of the new company as the Prussian Mining and Iron Works Company (Preussische Bergwerks-und-Hütten-Aktiengesellschaft) in Düsseldorf on 12 March 1866. The Irish shareholders were joined by some of Mulvany's business friends, including Gerson von Bleichröder and Wilhelm Conrad, both bankers, as well as Dr F. Crome, Lübeck, a lawyer, Gustav Arndt, a factory owner in Dortmund and Adolph Godeffroy, a merchant from Hamburg. The two mines were close together near the town of Castrop and he registered them under the name 'Erin'.

Henry Bewley, a Quaker, was the sixth son of Samuel Bewley, a shipowner and founder of the Bewley dynasty in Dublin. His brother, Charles, broke the state monopoly of the British East India Company in 1833 and chartered the *S.S. Hellas* to take 2,000 chests of tea direct from Canton to Dublin. In a few months, he was supplying almost half of the tea requirements of Ireland. Henry was partner in Messrs. Bewley and Evans, chemists, and then in Bewley and Draper which traded in diverse materials like mineral water and gunpowder as well as ink, sponges and toothpaste, and insurance.

He was very successful in financial affairs but was said to have made and lost fortunes three times. He invested in *gutta percha* which was used to insulate the first transatlantic telegraph cable laid between Valentia, Co. Kerry, and Newfoundland. He is also credited with having been the major investor in the cable company itself and it is believed to be family tradition that he received the first message to be transmitted at the Bewley breakfast table in Willow Park, the family home in Dublin. However, he went bankrupt later following the failure of Overend and Gurney, the private bank in London.

Mulvany, in his capacity as president of the supervisory board, noted at the initial board-meeting on 17 September 1866, that the company 'was financially well placed and possessed sufficient capital reserves to carry out future plans'. This acquisition was crowned with early success. Two additional shafts sunk revealed reserves of high quality coal suitable for gas, heating and coke, some of it better than anything yet found in all Westphalia. They also discovered material which was ideal for making refractory bricks then needed for lining blast furnaces. The new mine was also linked with a railhead to the Köln-Minden line.

A novel form of vertical integration was now available and the iron ore in the Westerwald could be used in the three blast furnaces at Vulkan, fired by coke from Erin. However, the difficulties of the economy were still causing problems in 1873–74. The cost of smelting iron had more than doubled in two years. In the autumn of 1873, the price of iron from the furnaces in the Rhineland dropped to the extent that some facilities were merely working to stock. Like other companies in the sector, the Prussian Mining and Iron Works Company was badly affected even if the mine itself was doing reasonably well. Castrop became the first town in the Ruhrgebiet to have street lighting supplied by gas from Erin.

The fact that the company had acquired its assets at low cost probably ensured that it could continue trading. However, in late 1876 the creditors became impatient. The company had accumulated debts of approximately 14 million marks.

Mulvany and his friends were able to draw up a plan to save the company and this involved drastic re-organisation. The plan was put before the Irish shareholders at a meeting in Dublin on 15 January 1877, but they refused to agree it. On 5 February the company went into receivership at Dortmund District Court and in December the Berliner Handelsgesellschaft acquired the assets.

During the eleven years of operation under Irish control, the project achieved good results initially but the blast furnaces in Duisburg were not enhancing the profits of the whole company and shared the fate of other iron producers in the region. Whatever expertise Mulvany had acquired in the mining and marketing of coal, he had very little technical experience in the smelting business. The bank quickly disposed of the furnaces, but the Erin mine remained dormant for some time. Eventually Friedrich Grillo, a successful businessman from Essen, acquired Erin for the sum of 40,000 marks and invested substantially in refurbishing the mine.

Even after the take-over, there were problems with exploiting

Erin's coal reserves. Unlike many of the other mines in the region, the seams were not horizontal, but closer to a 45-degree slope which made work very difficult. In addition, on several occasions there was serious ingress of water and many of the galleries were flooded causing the loss of equipment. Nonetheless, the mine survived and developed. It was worked until 1983 when it closed with the loss of over 3,000 jobs. Today, its 68-metre hammerhead pithead tower, a proud example of mid-nineteenth century steel construction, is the centrepiece of a memorial park dedicated to the Erin project which was the basis of Castrop's industrial development. Nearby, one administration building has been named the 'Mulvany Centre'.

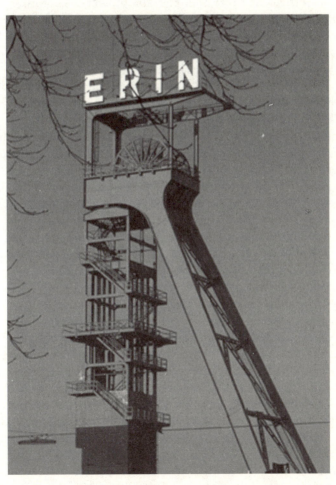

The original tower of the Erin mine, Castrop-Rauxel, preserved as a memorial

15

Mulvany's Interest in International Communications

William Thomas Mulvany was a man of great energy and interest in all matters relating to trade, industry and the infrastructure. As a foreigner, however, he remained aloof from any participation in politics, yet he was able to influence the course of developments in many sectors. He was a catalyst in the transfer of knowledge and experience relating to the industrial revolution in Britain. He was considered an expert on many matters in trade and commerce as well as monetary policy and was regularly consulted by bankers and politicians, despite the Erin fiasco.

On 20 November 1858, fifty industrial and mining companies met in Dortmund to establish the 'Bergverein' – the Mining Association. The founders included the National-Liberal Parliamentary deputy, Dr Hammacher, W. T. Mulvany, Edmund Heinzmann, Mining Engineer von Velsen, Hugo Haniel and other coal-mine proprietors. The association consisted of 89 members employing 15,857 workers. The objectives were to further developments in the mining industry in technical, economic, legal, administration and social matters. The further expansion of markets was a priority. Mulvany played a major role in this field right up to his death, becoming an honorary president on his retirement. Dr Hammacher said, 'Nobody worked as much as you did in the association to achieve its aims, especially the widening of the markets. In all important issues you were the teacher and master in all things, a courageous pioneer.'

The association concerned itself with a campaign for lower freight costs on railways and canals for essential raw materials such as coal and iron. Many of the large mines had no rail connection and many roads were in poor condition. Coal had to be transported by horse-drawn carts to the railheads. Through Mulvany' efforts it was possible in 1859 to sell Hibernia coal on the Dutch market. He spent considerable time in Holland working out agreements with the Holländisch-Rheinische Railway directors for special tariffs for regular goods trains from the mines to destinations in the Netherlands.

In 1860, Mulvany, accompanied by his son Thomas, led a delegation of the Prussian Coal Commission to London and the English and Scottish collieries. The visit took over two months and was obviously planned and organised by him. The aim was to see developments at first hand in handling coal as well as to inspect railway facilities and the running of the ports. The visit was a success as it revealed clearly the substantial differences between England and Prussia in the management of coal resources and its marketing in world markets. Prussia had a long way to go to equal the efficiency seen in Britain and the facilities in German ports were primitive by comparison. One member of this delegation who later occupied an important position in the industry, Dr Albert Serlo, kept a diary of their travels. Of the Mulvanys he said:

> Young Mulvany is a beef, an Englishman, through and through, the high, round hat pushed back, holding egotistically that only things English are good and useful, and all others, especially German, are ridiculous. He is, however, very helpful and assists us always regarding problems with the language and our ignorance of the city.
>
> The older man who accompanies us in order to introduce us in England, is kindness personified, he is helpful in every way possible and treats us as little children to be guided at every step.

In Scotland, the housing for miners and social services came in for favourable comment. Britain was then exporting coal to many countries and how this was organised was of special interest. During the two months, a formidable corpus of information was gleaned in discussions with directors of the collieries and government officials. In retrospect, the whole idea of such a visit was quite a brilliant move on Mulvany's part for the delegates had discovered for themselves what needed to be done in the Westphalian mines in order to make them competitive in world markets.

In his first memorandum dated 8 May 1868, on the coal and iron industry, Mulvany stressed the importance of the interdependence of railways and mines, not only for the mining industry itself but also for many other industries requiring raw materials at a reasonable cost. He pointed out that high transport costs were preventing Prussia from emulating the economic developments taking place in England and in America. His 'Stuttgarter Memorandum' of 1870 promoting the idea of a freight rate of 'a pfennig a mile' for certain materials, was taken up but only in northern Prussia at first.

He deplored the fact that Prussia's production of iron was minimal compared with that of other countries and exports were negligible while imports were substantial. Production costs were much higher than those in Holland, Belgium and England.

In the thirty years after Mulvany's demise, leading up to 1914, coal became an even more important national and strategic resource. After the armistice of 1918, the major aim of the allies, particularly of France, was to deprive Germany as far as possible of any benefits of these natural resources. A sharp analytical and critical insight into this period was made in 1919 by John Maynard Keynes:

> The delicate organisation by which these people (of Europe) lived depended partly on factors internal to the system. The interference of frontiers and tariffs was reduced to a minimum and not far short of three hundred millions of people lived within the three empires of Russia, Germany, and Austro-Hungary. The various currencies, which were all maintained on a stable basis in relation to gold and to one another, facilitated the easy flow of capital and of trade to an extent the full value of which we only realise now, when we are deprived of its advantage. Over this great area, there was an almost absolute security of property and person.
>
> The factors of order, security and uniformity, which Europe had never before enjoyed over so wide and populous a territory or for so long a period, prepared the way for an organisation of vast mechanisms of transport, coal distribution, and foreign trade which made possible an industrial order of life in the dense urban centres of new population. This is too well known to require detailed substantiation with figures. But it may be illustrated by the figures for coal, which has been the key to the industrial growth of Central Europe hardly less than England; the output of German coal grew from 30 million tons in 1871 to 70 million tons in 1890 and 100 million tons in 1913. Round Germany as a central support the rest of the European economic system grouped itself and on the prosperity and enterprise of Germany the prosperity of the rest of the continent depended.
>
> *(The Economic Consequences of the Peace by John Maynard Keynes, London, 1919.)*

16

Europe's Railways

In September 1873, Mulvany wrote and published a memorandum entitled: 'International Traffic in North and West Europe Facilitated by the New Ports at Vlissingen'.

Before writing this document, Mulvany had visited nearly all the ports along the North Sea coastline from Boulogne to the Elbe. Now that he had retired from full-time work, he had the opportunity of reflecting on the potential for future economic development of the continent as a whole. Communications, transport of people and goods were key issues, he was convinced, and he was highly critical of certain trends which he felt might stultify proper development.

A serious impediment, in his view, was the piecemeal planning and construction of relatively short stretches of railways primarily serving regional requirements. This was mainly because they were in the hands of private enterprise with limited capital resources and an eye only for the quickest returns and little thought for the good of national economy.

He kept himself fully informed on what was happening in other countries, travelling frequently to Belgium, Holland and England. The summer of 1873 saw him in Romania where he visited coal-mines and blast furnaces. In his view, the Romanians were capable of producing the best railway track steel.

Commercial intercourse between the nations could best be served by the construction of direct rail links right across the continent to carry express trains from London to St Petersburg and Constantinople. Essential to this development would be large, deepwater harbours on both sides of the Channel and North Sea. At the time of writing this memorandum, Mulvany was aware that few of the existing harbours on the eastern seaboard of the North Sea were ideal. Most suffered from the limitations of tides and in winter many were ice-bound. In Belgium, much effort had been put into developing Antwerp as a deep-sea port on the Scheldt River. It was well inland and necessitated the building of large wet docks. Taking a view that was contrary to that of many critics, Mulvany said that Antwerp would one day become one of Europe's major ports.

However, he saw even more potential in the then relatively small harbour at the mouth of the Scheldt, in Flushing on the island of Walcheren. This had the advantage of an inner and outer harbour, with the outer one having sufficient depth at all stages of the tide. Through friends in Holland, he was invited to study the plans for the expansion of this port. He was excited by the prospects for its future and how it might contribute to a grand plan for fast transcontinental passenger traffic.

He thought the plans for Flushing were too modest. He suggested greater expansion of the outer harbour and berthage. These he clearly delineated in the map he drew to support his point of view and obtained statistics, which he incorporated into his memorandum. These related to ferry services operating across the Irish Sea between Kingstown and Holyhead in the years 1860 to 1872. Four mail steamers worked this route averaging four connections each way each day. Sailing time averaged 3h 55m. Allowance was made for occasional delays due to storms and fog. If one examines this table which Mulvany drew up in 1873, there does not seem to be all that much of a difference in the duration of crossings by mailboat up to fairly recent years.

In this memorandum, Mulvany discussed the existing problems of the rail systems of the day. He deplored the absence of state-owned and state-managed railways and a concept for long distance lines connecting with those of neighbouring countries. Years before he had been critical of the slow pace of expansion of the railways in his own country. He urged more international consultation in planning new networks and held out for a minimum of two sets of tracks for all express routes. It was his view that respective systems should complement each other as far as practicable. In this manner of international co-operation, much could be accomplished in the realms of goodwill, commerce and peace, he suggested:

> In the important question of transportation the thought of a general or international concept appears to have been given little consideration or attention. Every country has its own, or to be more precise, no plan at all. When one examines the railways of Europe one finds even inside each individual country up to now very few stretches that indicate a prior general plan with one exception, perhaps, that of France, where centralisation and radiation (on the basis that Paris is France) reveal clear and specific signs of a plan that was considered well in advance.
>
> In England, originally there was no plan, not even a railway law. The railways were set up by companies which looked only to their

own advantages and correction of this only took place later under the pressure of strong competition between a multitude of companies.

In Prussia the numerous small states created a similar situation but with the unification of the country under Bismarck things changed for the better. Geographically, Prussia was well placed to allow the construction of long distance systems in all directions of the compass and the transport of coal and iron ore between Prussia and her neighbours allowed a fast pace of development.

Mulvany complained that even with the faster trains then running a traveller or a letter from London to Berlin took at least 30 hours, to Düsseldorf 21 hours, while the shortest possible route from London should take only 16 hours. If he were alive today he would be surprised to see that while passengers can now travel these distances in a matter of hours, letters might take even longer than in the 1870s!

The Prussian Mining and Iron Company participated at the Vienna Fair in 1873

17

Mulvany and the Infrastructure

The internal technical problems of his own industry by no means monopolised Mulvany's waking hours. He found ample time to become engaged in macro-economic affairs. In 1860, in his memorandum on transport, he had taken the first public steps to force the railway companies to introduce special tariffs for bulk transport of coal. He coined the phrase 'ein Zentner, eine Meile, ein Pfennig' – one hundredweight, one mile, one pfennig. With this as a slogan, he campaigned against the companies and lobbied government and political parties. Using facts and figures which he himself gathered, he analysed what he felt to be the great anomaly of British coal being sold at the same price or cheaper than Westphalian coal in the north of Germany and in Berlin.

Mulvany vigorously pursued this campaign and in the end was successful. He achieved substantial concessions at this early stage in the life of the industry, and coal was transported at a more acceptable rate. The principle of subsidised freight rates for essential commodities in certain regions was established and remained in force until recent times.

The shipment of coal on the Rhine rose from 500,000 tons in 1860 to 930,000 tons in 1868 whereas the tonnage transported by rail was only 300,000 tons. He proposed that with the special tariff policy and more rationalised loading facilities, i.e., more mechani-

The steamship Thomas John Mulvany, *about 1880*

sation, in the inland ports of Duisburg, Ruhrort, Hochfeld and Rheinhausen, with optimal use of the rolling stock, i.e., less standing time, the volume of exports could be substantially increased. He was conscious of the strong position British coal had won in the Belgian and Dutch markets despite the long sea passages. Largely through Mulvany's efforts, the imports of British coal dropped significantly. In Berlin in 1863, 1,509,940 tons of British coal were imported but by the following year it dropped to a third of this volume.

He gave considerable attention to the design and construction of larger vessels for the Rhine and the canals and corresponded with engineers and shipbuilders in Britain on the design of engines and boilers for these boats. Together with a few friends he ordered four Rhine freighters, one of which bore the name of his father, and by the 1890s they were operating on the Rhine.

In 1868 his memorandum, 'Deutschlands Fortschritte der Kohlen- und Eisenindustrie in der Abhängigkeit von der Eisenbahn' (Germany's Progress in the Coal and Steel Industry and her Dependence on the Railways), he considered Germany's future role within Europe and this demonstrated his ability to take a long-term view of inter-related if not integrated economics. He stated that coal, iron and a good transport system were mandatory prerequisites for all industries and cited the case of England as an example of a country which, more than anything else, could attribute her prosperity and power to these resources. Prussia was well endowed, he said, with similar resources for the first two but exploitation left much to be desired. Up to then Prussia was unable to compete with either England or Belgium in these raw materials and this was mainly due to long and costly transport and the actual distances between resources and the ports.

By present-day evaluation, the techniques employed by Mulvany in his position as chairman of a sub-committee of the Dortmund Association to promote a better awareness of Westphalian coal would be deemed appropriate and very advanced. Their first task undertaken was to stress the quality of the product and to compare it with coal from Wales for its calorific value. While Welsh coal was transported to Cardiff for up to 1.70 marks per ton and coal to Newcastle for up to 2.19 marks per ton, it was costing the mines in the Dortmund region up to 6.30 marks per ton to Bremerhaven. On average German coal transport cost was 4.84 marks per ton higher. British bunker coal could be bought in German ports at a price differential of 1.75 marks per ton.

Mulvany and his sub-committee next looked at the markets in

Scandinavia where they were able to develop interesting new outlets. Later Mulvany began to seek additional markets in Switzerland, Russia and Italy. He also suggested the construction of railways in China in the hope that this would provide additional markets in the long term.

Of all the groups to which Mulvany belonged, the most important one to him was the one which he co-founded, the 'Verein zur Wahrung der Gemeinsamen Wirtschaftlichen Interessen in Rheinland und Westfalen' (the Association for the Promotion of Common Economic Interests in the Rhineland and Westphalia). Chancellor Bismarck was well informed about this association but he could never remember its name so he referred to it in the Reichstag as the 'Langnam-Verein', the Long Name Association. This appellation stuck. It was founded in Düsseldorf on 10 October 1871, and held its inaugural general meeting in the Städtische Tonhalle on 15 November. The administrative office was located at Königsallee 34, now Düsseldorf's prestigious shopping mile. The principal aims were the co-ordination of efforts to develop industrial output and infrastructure, especially in the areas of transport of raw materials and finished goods, then considered as being chaotic. Mulvany was elected president. It was about this time that the first 'Kohlentag', a meeting of mine owners from home and abroad, was held in Düsseldorf. The meeting was described by Josef Winschuh in his book on the association:

> At this meeting the president of the Long Name Association played a generous and convincingly leading role. Through a generous and well-prepared discourse about the causes of the coal crisis and its solution to an eighty-man gathering he displayed the authority which he has long held among the personalities within the coal-mining, iron ore, and finance sectors. Assisted by a rich experience gained at home in the progressive economy of Great Britain, he developed an infrastructural programme which was later, to a great extent, realised by the development of the German railways. Explanations appeared sensible, and, by virtue of their being factual, urge reasonableness. One does not detect the impulsive, explosive Irishman in Mulvany but the British-trained, technically qualified and economically experienced spirit. Here is realism that is germane to the sense of reality of Westphalian industrialists and Prussian officials but with intuition, his calculation on a grand scale and the prospects for further development stands out and leads. Already in the correspondence which Bertelsmann (a textile manufacturer in Bielefeld) and Natorp had with Mulvany is the frank, obvious confidence which one has in the leadership ability of this man from a foreign land.

The association, whose members believed in the liberal theories and principles of Adam Smith, took a very vigorous stand on issues and problems facing the business community. It was most critical of the private railway system, which was regarded as an *imperium in imperio* and wielded an unacceptable power over manufacturing industry. Three main guidelines were set out, *viz*:

1. Fearless, energetic and unrestrained competition with all its problems
2. Strict and continuous governmental control
3. Agreements and understandings between participants in the economy for the general good.

In recognition of his work in this and other bodies, Mulvany was awarded the Kaiser's Gold Medal in 1875 and this award is cited on his gravestone.

In time, the Long Name Association began to wield a much wider influence on the commerce and trade of the region. In 1878, one of the most controversial questions being debated was free trade. The principles of Cobden in England found wide support in Prussia, especially among importers and traders in the strongly traditional Hanse families in Hamburg, Bremen and Lübeck. These families had links with overseas partners going back over centuries.

Mulvany and some friends took a determined stand against what they regarded as unqualified free trade, especially in the coal and iron sectors. There was an equally strong view taken by other sections of the community. In a letter to Axel Bueck, secretary of the association, on 1 December 1878, Mulvany wrote:

> England, as I foretold, is giving up free trade and even Gladstone begins to open his eyes. It is full time for Germany to awake.

However, the vice-chairman, Bertelsmann, found difficulty in aligning himself with the association's stand and resigned. Mulvany held him in very high regard and made strenuous efforts to dissuade him from leaving. The following resolution was passed:

> In consideration of the fact that the association owes its existence and great success to its vice-chairman Bertelsmann, the members, board and committee members owe him a very special thanks and empower President Mulvany to extend the urgent request to withdraw his resignation.

Bertelsmann continued in office but resigned the following year when Bismarck introduced protective tariffs.

The association articulated responses to many proposed laws and regulations. Nationalistic aims did not preclude the support and development of foreign trade relations. On 20 August 1880, the British Iron and Steel Institute was invited to hold its annual general meeting in Düsseldorf with the aim of improving trade links and mutual understanding on an international level. Mulvany was at the centre of arrangements for this event. He remained president of the association for 12 years until poor health forced him to step down.

18

A Man of Means and Influence

The Mulvany household in Düsseldorf numbered seven persons. The first child, a daughter, had died in Ireland in 1849 at the age of fifteen. Thomas James Mulvany, the father of W. T., had died four years earlier, and his widow, Mary, came to live in Düsseldorf, where she died in 1865.

There were three other daughters, Mary, Alicia Anne and Annabella. Alicia was disabled and confined to a wheelchair for the last 18 years of her life. The nature of her illness cannot be gleaned from the records. Annabella inherited the family talent for painting. Alicia devoted much time to writing poetry of a simple style and together with her sister Annabella and their maids, Annie MacDonald and Louisa McGuerin, she travelled by train on many journeys to Italy, Switzerland, the south of France and to many spas in Germany in later years. All of these journeys were described in verse form and a collection was published posthumously under the title 'Notes on the Journey'.

Thomas Robert, the only son, was active in the mines from the age of 16, under the guidance of his father and his uncle, Thomas John, who was technical director of Shamrock and Hibernia. Thomas Robert and his wife took up residence in Haus Goldschmieding and the estate, under his management, became a centre for racehorse breeding and the famous steeplechase meetings.

Unmistakable evidence of nepotism appears from time to time, both in Ireland and in Germany. It was the age of family businesses, families were large, provision had to be made for children's careers and there was a need to ensure continuity of investment holdings. Nephews of James Perry were given jobs down the mines, though they did not remain there very long.

Quite a number of Irishmen, some relatives of the shareholders, were brought over and given employment on the administrative level of the business while a group of manual workers from Ireland were employed down the mines. Over the years, some of the English workers and their families returned home.

The Mulvany family home in the Pempelfort suburb of Düsseldorf was more like a small schloss. It was set in an enclosed park with

T. J. Mulvany's residence at the Shamrock mine in Herne

Shamrock coat-of-arms above the entrance to T. J. Mulvany's Herne residence

many trees and gardens. A contemporary painting depicts Mulvany greeting some guests as they alight from a carriage. Unfortunately, the whereabouts of this painting today is unknown, despite a diligent search.

When the second shaft of Shamrock II was sunk and the site expanded, a large residence was built for the younger Mulvany brother. This was a three-storey redbrick building trimmed with cut stone. Thomas John was responsible for all technical matters and Louis Christian König assisted him. They were also very close friends, and later both emigrated to New Zealand.

The mansion has been maintained in excellent condition over

the last 130 years. Today, the Deutsche Steinkohle AG occupies the site which is dominated by the refractory towers of a refinery and chemical plant as well as large administrative buildings. The Mulvany residence survived the bombing in the Second World War and recently has been extensively and tastefully refurbished in its original style. The ambience is redolent of mid-nineteenth century German architecture and many of the furnishings date back to the seventeenth century. Nowadays, this splendid residence is mainly used for representational and educational purposes.

In 1872, after the purchase of the two mines in Castrop and the Vulkan blast furnaces in Duisburg, he was able to purchase a large estate just outside Castrop. Gut Goldschmieding was a fourteenth century residence complete with a round tower. Originally, it belonged to a nobleman, Johann von Scheel and the purchase price was 300,000 marks. His purchase of Haus Goldschmieding and its surrounding land placed him quickly among the wealthy and nobility of Westphalia and Prussia. The estate is situated on a height overlooking the town of Castrop (now united with Rauxel). It is rich, undulating parkland with a commanding view of the estate and the town, in the centre of which the original tall green tower of the Erin mine may be seen.

Haus Goldschmieding is a very solidly-built mansion with walls over one metre thick. It contains a splendid main hall dominated by a carved marble renaissance fireplace as well as a 'Knights' Hall' on the first floor. A large duck pond with black swans enhances the environment.

Mulvany had a massive double door in German oak installed during his occupancy. It is finely carved with garlands of shamrock. There are three panels cut in relief. On the right is the coat of arms of Westphalia, a stallion raised on his hind legs. On the left is the 'maid of Erin,' a well-endowed winged female with harp. In the centre is a raised right hand clasping a sword very similar to the coat of arms of the O'Brien's of Thomond ('Láimh Láidir Uachtar').

Clearly, Mulvany had a interest in the use of coats of arms. How the symbol of the O'Briens came to be carved on this door in Castrop is open to conjecture. Mulvany had spent years working on the drainage of the Shannon and its tributaries and he prepared the legislation for the navigation laws. He lived for a time at No. 5 Catherine Street in Limerick and being a religious observer he may well have worshipped at St Mary's cathedral. This church was founded by Domhall Mór O'Brien in 1194, was originally Catholic, and is famous for magnificent carved oak stalls on the high altar. There is

Haus Goldschmieding, Castrop-Rauxel

The living-room with its carved renaissance fireplace

Carved oak panel – symbol of Ireland – on the door of Haus Goldschmieding, Castrop-Rauxel

a possibility that the memory of these carvings lingered in Mulvany's mind when he commissioned the door in Westphalia. More than a century and a half later there is not a blemish on its surface. When Thomas John went to New Zealand, he took with him some family silver that was later divided between his descendants. Engraved on these items is this same raised right hand and sword and this cutlery is still being used today.

The Westphalian state region is famous for its wild horses. When Mulvany moved here he was able to indulge an interest in breeding and racing horses. As he did not have personal expertise, he arranged to procure it elsewhere and brought over James Toole, an authority in bloodstock in Ireland, and set him up in Goldschmieding. With his help, he laid out a course on the grounds with a distance of about three English miles. It was Prussia's first steeplechase course with 'Irish walls', high hedges and double hedges, wide water jumps and gates which went up hill and down dale.

The course was laid out in a rough circle around the Mulvany estate and was equipped with two grandstands, a saddling enclosure, a spectators' area on a hill which provided a clear view of most of the course, and a large parking area for coaches and carriages, etc. James Toole took part in the first race and later acted as starter until his death in 1896. Today, the racecourse is a large recreation area but the original fences may still be identified though they are now lines of close-planted trees.

The steeple-chase course on Mulvany's estate, with the mine in the background

A painting of James Toole starting a race

The first Castrop Races were held on 31 July 1875, attracting up to 30,000 spectators and continued to be held except for breaks during the two world wars, until 1968 when attendances of 50,000 were usual. In the early years the racehorses were entered by leading members of the Prussian nobility, many of whom also rode their own horses. In the archives in Castrop-Rauxel there is a painting of the start of a race at Goldschmieding. James Toole is seen with six horses and the jockeys are all members of the Prussian nobility.

James Toole supervised the stud on the estate and stallions were brought over from Ireland to cover Westphalian mares. The fees were 60 marks for thoroughbreds and 30 marks for others. One of the leading stallions standing at Goldschmieding in 1875 was 'Sprig of Shillelagh', a father of 'Donnybrook' and 'Erin-Go-Bragh'. Other Irish horses were 'Little Agnes', 'Little Wonder', 'Bandy', owned by Thomas Robert Mulvany, 'Ardpatrick', 'Gallopin Lassie', 'Crack-Tally-Ho' and 'Lady Tempest'.

During the races, over several days, work virtually stopped in the town and surrounding villages. Miners received time off and dressed in their Sunday best as did all other tradesmen and they flocked to the hilly course. Mulvany's expressed aim was to make the meetings an occasion for all classes of the community. He entertained numerous dignitaries and guests in the schloss and his pre-race breakfasts as well as the evening receptions were legendary. A typical menu was: Vol-au-vent, Roastbeef à l'anglaise, Cotelette de

Painting depicting the Mulvany family 'on Sunday morning'

Poisson, Perdreaux, Plum Pudding, Diabletines, Fruits et Desserts, accompanied by choice wines of the Rhineland.

The Berlin sporting magazine *Der Sporn* commented:

> ... We do not doubt that with the passion and expertise of Mr Mulvany, who is mainly responsible for the organisation of the Castrop Races, everything possible was done in order to meet the wishes of the horse owners taking part.

The jubilee magazine for one of the meetings included advertisements from Messrs Elliman Sons, Slough, for their animal medicines, such as 'Royal Embrocation', Messrs Duville & Co., Belfast, for their whiskey as well as Mangold Bros, Düsseldorf, for English gentlemen's clothing and travel goods.

Thomas Mulvany's interest too in horses and racing made him a well-known personality in Castrop. In the town centre there is a water fountain and a pillar with a horse and jockey to commemorate the heydays of the sport. Thomas later moved to Düsseldorf, to a house with the name 'Thionville', on Kaiserwerther Strasse. He was the British consul general until his death there in 1907. The house survived the bombing of the Second World War, is still occupied and situated not far from the headquarters of the conglomerate concern VEBA, which, following amalgamation with VIAG, in 2000 is now known as E-on. The Mulvany villa in Pempelfort did not survive the bombing and the area has since become built-up.

The Mulvany residence in Pempelfort, Düsseldorf
Painting by Wilhelm Christians

There is little information about the relationship of the shareholders to each other, apart from the rift between Mulvany and the older Malcolmson which became public knowledge. Mulvany and James Perry appear to have got on well. Perry at a later stage bequeathed over 20 of his 24 kuxen to the eight young children of his son-in-law, Marcus Goodbody, and the other 2 kuxen to his nephews John and James, if they remained in the mines. Using the excuse that the climate in Westphalia (or, perhaps, the mines) did not suit their constitution, they returned to Ireland and the shares were then transferred to the Goodbodys who were entitled to ownership on reaching their twenty-fourth birthday. The names were registered in the Grundbuch (Registry).

Annabella Catherine was born, probably in Limerick, in 1840 and lived in the Pempelfort villa until her death in 1917. She did not marry. Annabella was a generous supporter of Düsseldorf's Anglican community and left money and property to the church on her death. She also gave a number of paintings to the National Gallery in Dublin. The Pempelfort house was a popular social rendezvous for the Düsseldorf business circle whose members liked to mingle with British expatriates and practise their knowledge of the language.

Mary, her sister, married Hermann Seebohm, a mining engineer from Silesia, in Düsseldorf on 11 November 1875.

In 1878, George Vesey Stewart, an Ulster Protestant landowner, conceived the idea of an Ulster plantation in New Zealand. He persuaded the government there to allow a number of northern Ireland families, mainly farmers and members of the Orange Order, to take over unused land, formerly belonging to the native Maori inhabitants. Two vessels were chartered, the second of which was the *Lady Jocelyn*. She sailed with 238 passengers from Belfast on 20 May 1878, arriving at Auckland on 17 August.

Among the emigrants were Thomas John Mulvany, his wife and three daughters as well as Louis Christian König and Bernard McDonnell, both of whom had worked in the Erin and Shamrock mines. They were allotted land near Kati-Kati on the north island. Some, though not all, of the land was unsuitable for farming or it required investment to make it arable. The Ulstermen expected more support from their leader but Vesey Stewart was a persuasive populist rather than a practical pioneer. He promised more than he could provide or organise. It took several generations and much hard work to convert this land into a fertile region.

Even his descendants do not know what persuaded Thomas John Mulvany to emigrate to New Zealand. The fact that he was an engineer with mining experience and that gold deposits had been found in the north island suggesting that another Kalgoorlie was at hand may well have been an influencing factor. He was barely settled in when he began to write memoranda on the improvement of New Zealand's economy and developed the production of honey. He became the country's first bee-keeper with 138 hives and exported 5 tons of honey to the London market. The consignment crystallised *en route* and the venture failed. He died within four years of his arrival, aged 71, and is buried in Kati-Kati.

Photograph of staff taken on 6 January 1878, as a present for T. J. Mulvany – director of Hibernia, Erin, Hansa and Zollern mines – on his departure to New Zealand

> Memorandum written by T. J. Mulvany in New Zealand

NEW ZEALAND
Products and Manufactures.

SUGGESTIONS

AS TO THE SCOPE OF A PROPOSED ENQUIRY INTO THE BEST MEANS OF PROMOTING AND ENCOURAGING

MANUFACTURES AND LOCAL INDUSTRIES
IN THE COLONY

(Reprinted from the 'Bay of Plenty Times).

BY

THOMAS J. MULVANY, C.E.,

FORMERLY DISTRICT ENGINEER TO THE BOARD OF PUBLIC WORKS IN IRELAND; MEMBER OF THE INSTITUTE OF CIVIL ENGINEERS, IRELAND; AND LATTERLY GENERAL DIRECTOR OF THE PRUSSIAN MINING AND IRON WORKS COMPANY; MEMBER OF THE ASSOCIATION OF GERMAN ENGINEERS; AND OF OTHER TECHNICAL AND INDUSTRIAL ASSOCIATIONS IN GERMANY.

Tauranga:
PRINTED BY G. VESEY STEWART, "BAY OF PLENTY TIMES" OFFICE.
1885.

Note: Wilhelm-Hermann Seebohm came from one of the first German community of Friends (Quakers). His brother John Seebohm (1839-1907) had a woollen mill in Manchester. A son of Mary and Wilhelm-Hermann Seebohm, Kurt (born 25 June 1870), also became a mining engineer and director of the Britannia Coal-mining Company in Seestadt, Bohemia. His son, Dr Hans-Christian Seebohm, born in 1903, was also a Mining Assessor in Gleiwitz. After the Second World War, he became Traffic Minister in Konrad Adenauer's first government in Bonn. He signed the international agreement for the construction of the Main-Danube canal which opened in 1992 and gave access from the North Sea to the Black Sea, a development that would certainly have met with the approval of W. T. Mulvany. He died in 1965 and was entitled to a state funeral, which his family declined. Hans-Christoph Seebohm was noted for his Sunday speeches on behalf of displaced Germans from Silesia. He always wore a golden shamrock in his buttonhole in remembrance of his connection with Mulvany and Hibernia.

19

Düsseldorf's Harbour and Main Railway Station

Two major issues were being discussed publicly around 1860 in Düsseldorf, mainly because of the rapid expansion of the city and its population growth – the building of a suitable harbour and the siting of a new main railway station.

When Mulvany came to Düsseldorf in 1855, the city had a population of 30,000. In the following fifteen years, it had expanded substantially and by 1880, it was 95,000. Three private railway companies had connections to the city, the Bergisch-Märkische Railway, the Köln-Minden Railway, and the Rheinische Railway. The stations were small and likely to be unable to cater for an increase in passenger travel.

Mulvany undertook an analysis of the potential for expansion and for the city's capacity to absorb further growth as well as the siting of stations. He held the view that the city was geographically ideally suited to become a major fulcrum of intercontinental rail traffic. He suggested that it would be prudent to expect a population of 300,000 and to plan the railways accordingly.

With this in mind he wrote a memorandum, the essence of which was to abandon the existing location of the bigger station and to move it further north where a larger site with ample room for expansion was located. This is the site of the present goods depot. He also proposed that the main station should not take the form of a terminus but should allow traffic to pass straight through. Another suggestion was the complete separation of goods and passenger traffic.

However, despite his well-founded arguments, the main station was built in its present site but town planners later stated that there was much merit in Mulvany's original proposals.

The Harbour in Düsseldorf

The Rhine at Düsseldorf takes a wide, almost semi-circular bend eastwards and westwards on its way north. As it reaches the south of the city the fairway narrows and the stream is faster as a consequence. Proposals had been published to build a large harbour at this point on the eastern bank. Mulvany objected to this idea and

The Mulvany plan for a canal and new harbour on the Rhine at Düsseldorf

drew up what he considered a much better plan. This would involve cutting a canal on the western bank with a length of three kilometres that would rejoin the river as it straightened out again opposite the present football stadium. The canal would cut five kilometres off the route and allow the building of wharves and warehouses on either side without disturbing the city, which was mainly placed on the eastern side.

It was an inspired proposal that found much support but not sufficient to have the plan carried through. After Mulvany's death, the harbour was built on the south side of the city.

The Canals

Another important question occupying the minds of industrialists, politicians and town planners was the development of the inland waterways and canals for commercial use. Many of the large rivers such as the Rhine, the Main, the Elbe and the Neckar were not regulated until late in the nineteenth century. The building of canals was far behind the progress achieved in Britain, France, Belgium and Holland. As in the early days of the mining industry the main reasons were lack of venture capital and co-ordination of the interested parties.

The Rivers Ruhr and Lippe, flowing through the main coalfields, were too shallow to function as commercial waterways. On 24 April 1856, a Dortmund committee placed before the Commerce Ministry outline plans for a canal to connect the mines with the Emscher river and the Rhine.

Mulvany, perhaps because of his own experience of canal planning and building, was soon called in to assist this group. He proposed that the canal then envisaged (later known as the Rhine-Herne Canal) should be extended to reach Dortmund and eventually be further extended to connect with the Ems river and then the North Sea. The government in Berlin was sympathetic to this plan but had problems in regard to its financing. It was not until 1873 that a government commission was set up with Mulvany as chairman to determine the feasibility of the project and come to a solution as regards finance and operation. The estimates for the first stretch from the Rhine to Dortmund were expected to be over 30 million thalers.

A big question was whether the project could be financed out of private funding or whether the state should take over full responsibility. The commission persuaded the government eventually that, as private interests would eventually benefit greatly from the canal, they ought to contribute at least part of the finance and that from the administration viewpoint as well as the organisational aspects the state would be best equipped to start and complete the project.

Mulvany and several other commissioners had a meeting with government ministries in Berlin on 16 February 1976, which resulted in the state providing half of the estimated funds required.

Mulvany's commission had the task of preparing projections, estimating the cost details, specifying the beneficial effects the project was likely to have on the region's economy and forecasting potential growth of traffic for the following decades. As a young man in his thirties Mulvany had been through this kind of exercise, albeit on a much more modest scale with the Shannon-Erne waterway. A future connection from Dortmund to the Ems would cost 58 million marks.

After Mulvany's death, work finally began on this great project. The canal was opened to traffic in 1899; proposals by Mulvany's commission for the opening of the Mittelland-Canal to connect with the Elbe were first realised in 1920.

In the matter of international traffic, Mulvany stressed that the German government, as owner of the Rhine from Holland to Switzerland as well as its tributaries, should use all its powers to ensure that this great European waterway from its source to the sea should be deemed an international seaway open to all nations' traffic. That status has since been achieved.

In the question of suitable craft for both inland and coastal traffic, Mulvany had much to say. He corresponded with naval architects in England and Scotland especially those who were recognised authorities on smaller freighters. After much research on this, he came up with plans for a suitable vessel of about 600 tons.

Although sailing vessels as far back as the tenth century had connected Köln and London, it was not until the fourteenth century that inland traffic from the Rhine to Amsterdam began to develop. At the end of the eighteenth century, the river was partly regulated and this took nearly 70 years to accomplish. It was only after 1816 that a depth of at least three metres was dredged in the fairway from Köln to the Dutch border. The first steamship from England made its way upstream that year.

Mulvany's memorandum of 1881, 'Deutschlands Wasserstrassen' (Germany's Waterways) foresaw the introduction of 1,000-ton freighters and his views on this were supported by leading figures in the shipping industry. Again, in 1884, he wrote a further memorandum on this subject, particularly mentioning Duisburg as having potential for future expansion as a port. Since then Duisburg has become the world's largest inland harbour. In 1885, the Rhein-und-Seeschiffahrtsgesellschaft zu Köln ordered three steam-powered vessels of about 600 registered tons and a draught of 2.7 metres. These were used in the first regular cargo services between Köln and London.

Mulvany Co-Founder of the Düsseldorf Stock Exchange
After the establishment of the Mining Association, efforts were made to correct a situation which had given rise to problems in the region. Each mine owner had his own price for coal and prices were

continuously going up and down. Generally, prices were lower than the 25 years earlier and, in any case, lower than in Britain. In England, coal did not have to be sold below the cost of its production due to the existence of the Coal Exchange where producers and traders met weekly thus preventing sudden fluctuations in price levels.

Mulvany and his colleagues established the first Coal Exchange in Essen in 1865. From his arrival in Düsseldorf in 1855, he had established good and close relations with bankers and financiers. Together with the industrialist Bueck and the banker and financier Christian Trinkaus, Mulvany established the Düsseldorf Stock Exchange in 1880. In a memorandum of 11 January 1880, he stated that while professional associations for individual branches of industry had their advantages, they were unable to determine market prices or to regulate relations between the producer and the customer.

During his years in Germany Mulvany was a prolific writer of memoranda and commentator on important issues, taking great care always to have the correct facts and figures. In all, 27 such memoranda were published. I succeeded in locating some of these and translated the most interesting one – written on the miners' first strike (Appendix I).

Shareholding in Hibernia
Over the years blocks of shares changed hands, although within the confines of the families and relatives of the original investors. The Malcolmsons, originally major investors, transferred shares to their sons, George and Fred. Mulvany's cousin, Sir Cusack Rooney, also became a shareholder.

Outside this circle, there was one other person involved – Ebenezer Pike, a shipowner from Cork. Henry Bewley was a large shareholder in the Erin project. According to a note written by Annabella Mulvany he was also a big investor in the first transatlantic cable connection.

20

Mulvany's Hour of Glory

In his years of retirement, Mulvany continued to be actively interested in many fields of enterprise. As was the custom in those days when one wished to propagate ideas or engage in public debate, it was usual to write a paper on the subject and have it printed and distributed privately. Mulvany's memoranda cover a wide spectrum of interests from ship design to international railway systems and freight costs as well as canals. A full list is given in Appendix V.

Not all the proposals put forward by the expatriate Irishman in Düsseldorf met with immediate approval and support. One of the last debates in which he involved himself was the controversy surrounding monetary policy and what became known as the 'Doppelwährung' (dual currency) movement. This had its origins in the decline of silver as an international currency from the 1860s onwards. Gold was the main currency and there was a downward trend in gold reserves and production.

Mulvany took the view that it was prudent to preserve both metals for international business and became a member of the German Association for the Dual Currency in Köln. He suggested that the dependency upon gold alone resulted in heavy losses for the English and Irish agricultural communities and he held the gold currency mainly responsible for the downward trends in coal prices over a decade. Support for a dual currency waned over the next few years and eventually disappeared completely.

In writing his memorandum on the subject, Mulvany displayed a lively interest in international financial affairs although at the time his health was no longer robust. On 15 March 1883, he was invited to visit the Shamrock mine where a new, deep shaft had been sunk. He was presented with an address of welcome in verse by a young 'gnome' (boy) which ran as follows:

Deiner Jugend Frühlingsblüthe
Spross hervor im Sonnenschein,
Welche grosse, hohe Wonne
Soll es meinem Herzen sein
In des Lebens Abendsonne
Deines Glückes mich zu freu'n,
Sei mir gegrüsst du Tag der schönen Feier,
An dem das Glück in Deine Silberhaare
Noch solchen sonn'gen Schein erzeust!
O, möchte Gottes heil'ger Vorsicht Walten
Noch lange Dich am Leben uns erhalten
In der Gesundheit Füll' und leidensfrei!
Der schönste Lohn, den edle Seelen finden,
Die in der andern Wohl das ihre gründen,
Der werde Dir in reichstem Mass zu Theil;
Denn Dein unablässig edles Streben
Verdient mit Recht ein ausgezeichnet Heil.
Sonnenschein auf allen Sohlen
Garantirt von Deinem Gnomen.

Glück auf!

Your youth's springtime flower
Blossomed out in sunshine
Which great high joy,
Should be in my heart
In life's evening sunshine
Your fortune for me to enjoy.
Be greeted day of happy celebration,
On which happiness still shines on your silver hair
O that God's holy care may prevail
And keep you long in our midst.
In full of health and free from pain!
The best son, whom pure souls find,
Who base their well being on that of others,
That may be granted to you in abundance,
Because your untiring noble struggle
Rightly deserves an outstanding salute.
Sunshine on all levels
Is guaranteed by your Gnomes
'Glück auf!'

This address is one of the few mementos to survive bombing in the Second World War. On the back of this address Mulvany scribbled a note:

> Presented to me by a gnome, a young German boy, in Zeche Shamrock, Flöz Sonnenschein, 1,376 or 1,578 metres below ground today, 15th March, 1883, as I went down there to view this magnificent and deepest pit on its completion.

William Thomas for his part was also capable of writing verse, as the following lines which he wrote in 1866 reveal:

Paraphrase for the miners

Eternal Father, Creator Great,
Whose will gave earth its glorious state,
Who out of chaos dark and deep,
Made land and sea their limits keep;
Oh bless and guard these men of thine,
From daily perils in the mine.
Oh, Thou whose voice the waters heard,
Save these brave miners by Thy word,
Midst all the dangers of their way,
Be Thou their guide, be Thou their stay;
Oh bless and guard these men of thine,
From daily perils in the mine.
Deep in the dark and lowly cell,
Most Holy Spirit with them dwell,
That they may see there is no place
Too deep or dark for Thy free Grace;
    Oh bless and guard these men of thine,
    From daily perils in the mine.
O Trinity of Love and Power,
Our brethren shield in danger's hour,
From rocks and blasting, fire and woe,
Protect them wheresoe'er they go;
    Then evermore these men of thine,
    Shall sing glad praises from the mine.

W. T. Mulvany's contribution as one of the founding fathers of the Rhineland's expanding economy was honoured at a crowded function held in Düsseldorf's Tonhalle on St Patrick's Day 1880, to mark his 25 years in Germany and his resignation after 12 years as president of the Long Name Association. It was a splendid affair with an orchestra playing *Tannhäuser* and other triumphant Wagnerian music. Mulvany received a number of specially designed trophies in silver and gold.

The meeting was presided over by Mulvany's long-time friend and Reichstag deputy, Herr von Hagemeister, who said 'the history of Rhineland-Westphalian industry would forever be linked with the name of Mulvany.' He listed many achievements such as the improved and economic transport, especially in the railways and canals, the modernisation and rationalisation of coal production that Mulvany personally had instigated.

In reply Mulvany reviewed his years in Germany and said:

> I believe that the future of Germany will bring considerable progress in political and material affairs and that soon one shall be able to place a hand on the map of Europe and point to the true Grande Nation. I have no doubt that in relation to the industry you will also be equally successful as in war. God grant that you will achieve this. For the new nations with their ever preparedness for war it is necessary that the country is rich and that there is much money there.

Wilhelm Funcke, his friend and confidant, said:

> When a man who as a pioneer in mining, in transport, and in freight costs, and in very many other economic affairs, moves in the form of a brilliant star, is, due to advancing years, unable to carry on in the office of president of our association, this news make me very sad indeed.
>
> ... Clear and pure as the waters of the mountain flowed, the work-filled life of a man in whose rich spirit the care of himself was the last thing.

On 30 October 1885, Mulvany lay dying in his house, 'Knappengut', in Pempelfort. A service was held in his room in the morning and he received communion. His daughter Annabella described the final hours:

> He blessed us all, including his grandchildren, about 2 o'clock the agony began and lasted twelve hours, he complained for the first time and said to the doctors that it was hard to suffer, but his spirit helped him to suffer this test. He took his leave of my mother with the words: 'My love, my love' with a look of enduring love. To my disabled sister Alicia Anna, he said 'Prepare to meet thy God, goodbye till the morning.' He did not speak until 10 o'clock that night then he saw my deeply sorrowing brother and said 'My boy'. At one o'clock I knelt at

his bedside and he said: 'My dear child'. A half-an-hour later his truly great soul was no longer under the living of this earth.

A few days later William Thomas Mulvany was buried in Düsseldorf's North Cemetery. His wife survived him by only three months. She and the other members of the family were later interred in the same plot. The graves are maintained in perpetuity by the City of Düsseldorf.

The Last Resting Place
The Mulvany plot forms a small part of the 'Ehrenfriedhof' or Plot of Honour where distinguished citizens have been laid to rest for generations. It is known as 'millionaires' hill' today because of the number of graves of industrial magnates. William Thomas, his wife Alicia, their second daughter Alicia, as well as his son Thomas and

The Mulvany Family plot – Düsseldorf, North Cemetery

wife are buried there. The plot of the Haniel family with whom William Thomas was closely acquainted is twenty metres away.

As was customary in the latter half of the nineteenth century, memorials were often decorated with verses as well as details of births and deaths. The Mulvany headstone is bordered with a garland of shamrocks in relief:

The inscriptions reads:

Alicia A. Mulvany:
'11 Timothy 11.3.4.'
Sacred to the memory
Of our beloved sister,
Alicia A. Mulvany.
2nd daughter of W. T. Mulvany,
born at Ardara, Donegal, Ireland,
October 19, 1835, died at Pempelfort,
Düsseldorf, Nov. 1st, 1898
Of whom the world was
Not worth.
Heb. X. 38.
W. T. Mulvany & his wife, Alicia
Goodbye till the morning W. T. M.

Sacred to the memory of our beloved parents
William Mulvany Esq.,
late Commissioner of Public Works, Ireland,
Inhaber der Preussischen Goldmedaille
für Gewerbliche Leistung,
Born 11 March, 1806 at Sandymount, Dublin,
died 30 October, 1885 at Pempelfort, Düsseldorf,
and his dearly beloved wife
Alicia née Winslow,
Born 2 April, 1797 at St John's Point, Donegal,
died 26 Feb., 1886 at Pempelfort, Düsseldorf, 1886.

Why so disquieted my soul
The night will soon be o'er
I see a light upon the path
From a far distant shore
Be strong and wait God's leisure
The time shall surely come
When the glorious band of Christians
Shall all be gathered home.

They loved their faithful shepherd
Who led them on the way
And with his rod he chastened
When their footsteps went astray.

The mortal conflict over,
The troubled waters cross'd,
But looking to the Saviour
No wanderer was lost.

In the presence of their God
They are satisfied and blest
They have reached the promised land
And gained their promised Rest.

A.M. nee Winslow.
Rev. 5.9.13.

Thomas Mulvany

Sacred to the memory of my beloved husband
Thomas Robert Mulvany, Esq.,

H.R.M.'s Consul General for Westphalia and
The Rhenish Province
22 July 1839 in Dublin, 16th August, 1907 in
Haus Pempelfort, Düsseldorf.
The memory of the just is blessed
Wherever I may roam and whatever fate betide
Thou'll never be forgot till I rest by
Thy side.

An obituary in the *Irish Times* of 5 November 1885 refers to Mulvany's appointment to the Ordnance Survey in 1825 and ten years later his involvement in the survey of the Shannon as district engineer:

> In 1841, he was selected by the late Field Marshal Sir John Burgoyne, chairman of the Board of Works to assist in the preparation of drainage and fishery bills for Ireland and to attend their progress through Parliament. The bills were passed in 1842 and he was appointed Commissioner of Drainage and Inspector of Fisheries and in 1847 made a Commissioner of Public Works.
>
> He was a Liberal in politics and a free trader, but from the experience acquired during his long residence in Germany he became, from conviction, a protectionist or, perhaps rather an advocate of 'fair trade'. Mr Mulvany was an Irishman of great energy and resource, who, before all things, looked to the advancement of his native land, and it is a suggestive commentary on our system that long experience and abilities of a high order, which should have been devoted to the amelioration of this country and the development of its resources, were more highly prized and rewarded in a foreign land.

The *Düsseldorfer Anzeiger* of 30 October 1885, published a statement from the Langnam-Verein:

> It is our sad duty to inform our members that the founder of our association and honorary president, Mr William Thomas Mulvany, has died. Born in Ireland, later a high-ranking English civil servant, he came to Germany thirty years ago and devoted his abilities in the coal and iron industries, to whose development and greatness he contributed an outstanding service. Up to the last days of his life, in untiring endeavours in the pursuit of rightly recognised aims, his great vision and wide horizon qualified him to assume a leading position in the Rhineland-Westphalian industry. Thus, he combined all the forces of the association that were called for during the difficult situation of the glorious war against France in order to promote common interests.

By virtue of his economic activities, closely allied with the new Fatherland, he had, as had her best sons, followed with pride and pleasure the growth of the power and greatness of the German Reich. His whole self was filled with the burning wish and endeavour to secure the consolidation and support of the economic and social foundations of the praiseworthy position and growth of the Fatherland.

The deceased was known and respected among a very wide circle. But those privileged to be close to him know that this man had great characteristics together with full sensitivity for everything beautiful an ideal, with incomparable kindness and unchanging personal gentleness towards all. This well-honoured name will be linked in the first place with our association as long as its activities in the history of the economic and social development will be recorded.

Düsseldorf, 30 October 1885
The Council, the Association for the Promotion of the Common Economic Interests in the Rhineland and Westphalia.

Postscript

The Hibernia coal-mine ceased producing coal in 1925 after 67 years in operation in which over 18 million tons were produced. The name Hibernia survived as Germany's largest generator of electricity until 1969. It was then amalgamated to form the fourth largest conglomerate in the country under the name VEBA.

VEBA's headquarters in Düsseldorf commemorates Mulvany's contribution to its origins by a bronze bust in the main reception hall. VEBA merged with VIAG, under the new name E-on, in 2000.

The Shamrock mine closed in October 1967 in the wake of yet another recession in the coal sector. It had produced 62.3 million tons of coal since its foundation.

The Erin mine in Castrop-Rauxel closed down at the end of 1983. It was then employing 3,800 workers. The pit-top tower of the mine with the name Erin on top has been preserved as part of a memorial park to honour the contribution Mulvany and his friends made to the development of the city of Castrop.

For many years (1900–1975) the city of Herne incorporated the shamrock (Kleeblatt) in its coat of arms. It was changed when the city expanded to incorporate a number of surrounding satellite towns.

Mulvany is remembered with street names in Düsseldorf, Gelsenkirchen, Herne and Castrop-Rauxel, where there is a street named after his son, Thomas Robert. There is no street name or memorial to commemorate Mulvany in his native Ireland!

Mulvany's Bequest to the City of Düsseldorf

In the later decades of the nineteenth century, a number of English workers came to work in the iron and textile industries as well as the mines in the Rhineland and Westphalia. In Düsseldorf an Anglican chaplaincy was established to cater for their spiritual needs. The linen industry in Bielefeld was helped by the skilled workers recruited in Belfast.

About 1875, W. T. Mulvany decided to set aside a small fund to build a church in Düsseldorf for the English Anglican community in the Rhineland. He designated a plot of ground within his own property in Pempelfort as a site. After his death, work began on a modest sized neo-Gothic building in Paderborn stone, located near Prinz-Georg-Strasse. It seated 250 and the pews were made in Sauerland oak. The campanile had a peal of 14 bells on which German and English tunes were played every evening.

Annabella Mulvany, the last surviving daughter, was very active in church affairs and, through her efforts, a large three-storey parsonage was built in 1909. When the war broke out in 1914, it was converted at her request, to an emergency hospital for wounded soldiers from the front. In her will, she bequeathed property shares, her furniture and 120,000 marks to the church.

The original Christ Church built on the Mulvany property, Düsseldorf-Pempelfort

On 11 June 1943, the US Air Force bombed Düsseldorf and Christ Church, which was close to a Gestapo barracks, was almost levelled. The tower remained standing as well as two-thirds of the chancel arch. The arch had borne the inscription: 'Glory to God in the Highest, Peace on Earth, Goodwill Towards Men'. The middle segment with 'Peace on Earth' disappeared in the rubble. After the war, at the instigation of the city authorities, the church was rebuilt on another site not far away on Rotterdamer Strasse, on the banks of the Rhine, close to the present International Fair Grounds. Opposite the church entrance is a parsonage with the name 'Mulvany House'. In front of the church is a bust in stone of the man from Sandymount.

Christ Church, built in the 1950s, to replace the original building destroyed in the Second World War. It serves the Anglican community in the Rhineland

Interior of Christ Church

Bust of Mulvany in the grounds of Christ Church, Düsseldorf

Appendix I

A Few Friendly Words to Employers and Employees, by Wm. T. Mulvany, Düsseldorf, 21st June, 1872

The Miners' Strike.
'Eine gelinde Antwort stillet den Zorn.'
A mild answer mollifies the anger.

A quiet, impartial and informed discussion on the relations between employers and workers and a friendly word to both is the most suitable means of dealing with the differences existing between them.

At some time this word will have to be spoken. Why not now at the outset!

Responsibility before God and the Fatherland, which all those carry who, in an active and passive manner, slow, delay, or prevent the wonder of progress in the great German nation in her industry and railways, the unification of all her members, which was won by the costly expenditure of the blood of her children on the field of battle, so that it would be crowned by a peaceful growth, appears to me to be so fearful that, through remaining silent, I at least do not wish to be a participant thereof.

Many, perhaps, will ask with what right do I as a foreigner have to appear as an intermediary and criticise my involvement. But exactly as such I have nothing to do with politics and adjudge the material situation from a practical standpoint, on the basis of 46 years' experience in the direction of large state organised operations of different kinds which provided thousands of men from all trades with employment and living, whereby I was always seriously exercised in promoting the interests of the workers and their dependents and without being a capitalist, to bring into being new companies which were able to improve the situation of the working classes in that they provided them with employment.

Having now lived for 18 years in Prussia, I and my friends have established five large collieries (Hibernia, Shamrock, Erin, Hansa and Zollern) in Westphalia and an important steel mill (Vulkan) in the Rhineland, and for the development and improvement of the mining industry as well as the support of the difficult role of the miner, I have done everything my modest powers allowed.

If I have succeeded even in a small way to assist in the magnificent development which enables the collieries and industries of this district to stand out from what they were in 1854 and which for all that time have served as exemplary, so may I turn to mine owners and the mine workers, especially those of experience and in the middle or older years who really understand their profession and who can recall the conditions then obtaining, and to request them to maturely consider without prejudice what I have to say here.

1. The experience of a long life has proved to me that where the work is free the best and true friend of the worker is the employer. Exceptions to this rule are very rare and only serve to prove the rule and the reason for this is quite simple, because the true interests of the employer are identical to those of the worker or as those of a father of a household and his family.

    The scenes of worry, which efforts, which risks, which sacrifices in money and health on the part of the employer I have witnessed in the course of my life, where it was necessary to obtain cash for the monthly or fortnightly pay day to pay wages irrespective of whether the work performed was profitable or not!

    Has one ever heard of sacrifices which the agitators, wherever or whoever they may be, have made for the workers whom they wish to advise without being invited? Are they helping the worker or his family out of their own pockets? Are they really helping him to purchase land, to build houses, or otherwise in order to improve the situation.

2. I cling to the basic principle: Luke, X, 7. 'A worker is worth his wage', and in that I understand the full value of his completed work, according to the market rate, which does not have to be measured according to the mood or the whim of the employer but which is measured according to the principle that in the honest execution of his duty the worker is not only put in a position of living a good and healthy life in the conditions of the country in which he lives according to his standing but also through wisdom and energy to achieve savings in order to improve his situation and to keep him when he can no longer work.

    But, upon reflection, everyone must appreciate that nature has ordained that we have strong men and weak, talented, energetic, and stupid and lazy, skilled workers and beginners, honest, ambitious, and conservative, and those who are the opposite; in short that men are not all alike, or ever will be and that is why it would be the most blatant and hurtful injustice against all good, hardworking, intelligent, and conservative workers whatever their standard, if they were to be paid the same wage as the other classes.

3. But, perhaps, one may say to me: Under such circumstances how can the full value for the work according to the market rate be established?

My answer is: Through the simple and generally prevailing law of supply and demand, which rates rule more or less all commercial enterprises where work is free in a free country, provided that there is no involvement of a third party between employer and employee and where no force or pressure exists on both sides.

The interest of the whole nation is too strong, too much integrated with the development of the nation's industry that any orderly country such as Germany would ever for one moment allow the use of force or pressure whether overt or covert on the part of the worker or the employer.

The question of the effect of the law of supply and demand as it applies in the special case of the miners will be dealt with further on.

4. What I should like to suggest is this: That in the interest of the workers and of all classes and especially the mine workers themselves the system of 'strikes' is not a suitable method of settling differences, that it unavoidably leads to the contrary step of 'lock-out' and that neither one nor the other should be allowed inside the borders of the German State wherein the working classes on the whole are better brought up, educated, and used to discipline, also in respect of the ownership of their own homes, in other words a community much better situated and therefore much better in a position to solve differences with the employer as in the region where the principle of the 'strike' evolved which, unfortunately, has been transferred it would appear perhaps only to affect the development of Germany in a sly manner.

Whatever the motive may be, I, as a practical and politically independent person, foresee that when all parties do not unite in order to exclude the system of strikes from this country it will be the nightmare of the domestic industry, leading to the decay of morality and discipline both in every branch of State and private business.

5. Already the strike system has deterred much capital in-

vestment from England and continues to do so. Over there are many wise, talented, and well-meaning people who have preferred to risk their capital in the distant colonies, in North and South America, and in the southern hemisphere than to expose their property to the continuous vagaries and themselves and their workers to the tyranny and uncertainty of the strike system which exists at home and if this whole system is not changed in the near future I am convinced that because of this England will lose its important position within the industrial nations.

Speaking from personal experience, for instance, I allowed myself to be induced and arranged also for my friends in 1854 and in the following years to invest substantial capital hereabouts, trusting in the orderly, calm and solid character of the German coal-miner and in the laws which governed our operations and which kept any thoughts of a local strike far from my mind.

Every man with some experience knows how well Belgium and Germany have competed with England in manufacturing in recent years; all that will end very quickly if the strike system takes hold in Germany.

6. The strike is a sharp, double-edged sword, which almost always first and most dangerously wounds those who wield it. This system is like the dog in the fable who allows the meat to fall out of his mouth in order to snap at his shadow in the water under him.

The first result of the strike for the worker is the immediate stopping of the wages, his income from which not only he and his family lives, but which enables him to purchase his needs from others who must suffer with him. In the case that we now have where the average wage per man, as is known, so high is that the total losses of these classes will be shocking, for what the number of those at present striking is considered, a loss of 20,000 to 25,000 thaler per day may be estimated. When and how will that be recovered? For the employer it is, up to a certain extent, more of a deferral of profit rather than a loss because he, as a result of the wilful use of the strike system by his workers, is, according to the provisions of his contract, regarding default, protected by the law.

The community and the whole industry of the Fatherland, with all workers in other manufacturing branches and their families, are suffering ten times more daily due to the shortage of raw materials which the folly of the workers keeps from them. How do the instigators of the strike justify these results which must become worse every day before the people who blindly follow them like a herd of sheep away from the even and simple and legal way of settling disputes down this illegal and false path?

One will say to me: These people have savings – or had their last wages in their hands – or they could live for several weeks on credit, or that they receive support from other miners not on strike and so forth. But I shall not allow myself to accept this and will see through all their arguments. They are not valid and only reveal in some cases that the strike is not due to a lack but to a surplus which would indicate that the wage rates are by no means too low.

Such arguments might come from the young, the hotheads, and single miners, but the experienced miner, the father of a family, will not be blinded by this. He will say that the credit will end when no daily income is there to cover it. He will also say to himself that other miners will not be prepared to deduct part of their well-earned wages from his family to support others not working for an uncertain period and when he is clever he will say to himself that he knows his own business best and is best able to judge the value of his own work. I will complete his answer when I say:

7. All these and other raisonnements cannot reduce the loss of assets of the worker nor of anyone else involved but will only render the general loss more painful insofar as they prove the falseness of the situation in which the worker finds himself because of the effects of the agitator for the strike.

Strikes are not only wrong but fully inappropriate for assisting the workers and they are unworthy of a free and educated worker in a free country, for he thus freely hands over his independence for the sake of a bad kind of tyranny. Only for slaves in a country where the right to employment is not recognised by law may excuses be found when they strike in order to force their employers against their will.

When the above considerations are brought to bear on strikes in general they are doubly valid in regard to the strikes of the coal-miners in the Prussian State, in which by virtue of the Mining Law the supervision of the Mining Office, the existence of the Knappschaftsverein (miners' social fund) with its statutes for the welfare of the miners and the large subventions of the trade and colliery owners, the relationship between employer and employee which is so fully organised and in such a friendly and familiar atmosphere than in other trades so that nobody may find a justifiable basis for the strike system. I know of no country in which the miner, from his birth to his death, is better protected under the present laws than under the improved laws in the coal-fields of the Rhineland and Westphalia.

8. Up to now, I have not expressed any view regarding the demands made by the committee which has called for the strike in the Essen region, but rather have spoken only about principles. I speak only of what I know and I do not know sufficient or nothing at all about the piece contract and the details of the wage structure and other agreements of the miners in the above region. What I say is this: When any miner has any reasonable grounds to be dissatisfied he should pursue the regulated way of discussion and negotiation with the management of the mine where he is employed and, if not satisfied, he should give 14 days' notice and then seek work in another mine but should not rely on the strike method.

9. However, I personally am well informed about the conditions, the statistics, and the management of the mines in which I hold shares; as many are aware I know these mines also in practice, and therefore, often inspect the work below the ground while my attention is also given to the wage, management and operating costs as matters of the utmost importance for the present and future welfare of our workers and the interests of our company, also the method of regulating the expanded trade in which we are involved.

10. It is by no means my intention to close the door on any complaint of the worker and still less to prejudge any special complaint against any mine. On the contrary, I vote for the thorough discussion of every individual case between the parties themselves and for this what is right always with the guiding regard for the welfare of the worker, but this should be under correct and healthy conditions as between parties in which both sides have an interest in peace and in friendship to work together and not between enemies who are opposed to each other, which will be unavoidable when the miners come up with a threat of a general strike from which up to now they have not washed their hands. Above all, every negotiation between individual mines and their work-

force should be based on known and specific principles which are compatible with healthy human understanding and which for every mature person are acceptable.

11. With regard to these principles which should form the basis of any agreement I beg to remark:

a) that, according to law, everybody is free to seek work in a mine under the existing conditions and factory regulations or not. When anybody who does not accept the conditions and takes employment in that particular mine and when, after a trial, he still finds that the conditions do not suit him he can, by giving 14 days' notice, leave the mine. In a district where there are many mines it is possible for everybody to find employment where the full value of his ability will be paid. When the conditions and regulations of a mine are really difficult or unjust, the management will soon find it necessary to change them in order to hold on to its workers.

b) That, as I have already shown under 2, not all men are equally talented (not everybody is a Bismarck or Moltke) and it would be absurd because of this to pay all workers the same wage or, as suggested by the instigators of the strike, to fix a normal wage. On the contrary, insofar as possible every worker should be paid exactly the value of his work.

Or would it not be absurd or unjust to pay a skilled and experienced hewer the same wage as that of a young, in-experienced apprentice?

c) That in the coal-mines and especially under the insurance law discipline, the strong and sharp discipline, is not only absolutely necessary for the work itself but also for the security of life and the property of those who are in ownership.

The mine owner must secure discipline under all circumstances, not only in the mine itself as well as in the vicinity above ground, and every miner should consider it his first duty not to allow anyone to transgress this discipline but to stimulate in his comrades and keep alive a sharp feeling for it.

With this principle of discipline, strikes and pressure as well as arguments and hectic disputes in the mine or tunnel or vicinity are not compatible. Prussia, through the discipline of her army, has given the world an example of how to succeed – should we in the collieries not give the same example?

d) That the conditions not only in every pit but also in many seams in the same pit are so different so that totally different agreements and regulations for those at the coalface and transporters are necessary so that it is simply nonsense to even consider a general price fixing or regulation on the part of the committee, it is rather a situation which must remain subject to the free agreement between employer and employee and should they not reach agreement at first the natural effect of supply and demand will very soon lead both parties to a mutual agreement.

However, I must here repeat that the agreement should not be measured mainly by the mood of one or the other of the parties but by the real value of the job to be done, i.e., that an able man who understands his job and who works with goodwill in accordance with the basic principles under paragraph 2 should be paid the correct wage for his work.

From my own practical experience I am in a position to claim that since the beginning of the agitation for the strike the productivity of the hewer has not only significantly dropped on several occasions but that the same with higher wages and otherwise equal conditions have decreased.

I can also claim that good hewers in 8-hour shifts have earned two thalers and over whereas others with the same agreement and the same conditions earned under 1 thaler 10 groschen, and even others did not earn more than 19 to 20 groschen per shift.

This shows that it is not possible to fix a norm for an agreement so that every worker, whether good or bad, skilled or otherwise, energetic or lazy, cannot earn the same wage but, as already indicated, must be paid for the value of the work performed. In fact, in agreement rates, as I know them, it is possible for skilled hewers, when they want to work just as their colleagues in Belgium and England, to earn 1 to 2 thalers and the best 2 thalers 10 groschen and over in an 8-hour shift.

I can also claim that the wages in the cases of which I have knowledge are substantially higher and 25% above that of two years ago.

The current production of coal, even when one does not include the interest charges on investment, is higher than the actual sales price of coal in the year 1864, where trade in coal is under normal conditions and this gives ground for much worry regarding the future of the coal industry.

As one will see, I view as the main factor the wage question for the hewer of the coal. The wage costs for transport and other expenses vary a good deal according to circumstances and without doubt mine owners in the future will use horses and machinery instead of men to move the coal.

I repeat here again that I will not allow myself to make any judgement of individual cases in the entire wage question but will rather refer to general principles and will only quote special cases and details where these are personally known to me.

e) The other demand put forward by the instigators of the strike, namely the 8-hour shift appears to me to be suitable, depending on the special situation of every mine for mutual and friendly agreement, provided that both parties are able to arrive at the proper attitude.

f) I would like to recommend to the mine owners to do everything possible to promote the trust between employer and employee; not to allow any change in the fixed agreement and factory regulations which would be less favourable to the worker without consulting the management of the mines and only when these have been settled three months in advance.

g) Above all I recommend that where agreements exist to the mutual satisfaction of the employer and the employee, in order to strengthen the trust of the latter, a premium system should be introduced by means of which for continuous and regular and punctual appearance for work and to these workers who earn the highest monthly wage based on the agreement premiums should be paid.

In this way the older and good workers will be convinced that their interests and those of the employer are identical and must go hand in hand; the younger workers and apprentices will receive a new stimulus to achieve higher productivity.

12. Finally, I may, in the interest of the country and especially in the interest of the worker himself, once again loudly and urgently recommend that the strike system, which, for free men is unworthy and only appropriate for slaves, as well as leading to its opposite, the lock-out, should be abandoned for all time, that every group of workers return to work and that then after about a week when a friendly atmosphere has been established, an understanding between the worker and the managements and mines will be reached on the basis of the principles which I have taken the liberty of setting out above.

So will the development of our great coal industry be brought back to the solid basis which has given our region the capability of competing not only with the whole world but also to play the role of the mother of intelligence and order and to win for Germany the highest place among the industrial nations.

Düsseldorf, 21st June, 1872
Wm. T. Mulvany

Postscript:
After the foregoing was written and sent for printing I have seen a report in the newspapers that in England which may claim the dubious honour of being the birthplace of the strike system, a union of 40,000 miners in the collieries of Durham at a meeting on the 15th of this month, after long and bitter experience, has, through its spokesman, strongly criticised the strike system and has decided that in future all differences such as were already there for over a year will be settled in a friendly manner and on the basis of the principles which I have referred to. May their good sense and the success in improving their situation since they have adopted these principles serve as an example to others and lead to an end of all strikes and lock-outs.

(Translation by John J. O'Sullivan)

Appendix II

Translation of Letter of Address to the chaplain of the Irish workers in Gelsenkirchen

Herrn Regierungsgeistlicher Schulrat Sebastiani

Reverend Sir,
We, the Irish Roman Catholics employed in the Irish Collieries at Gelsenkirchen and Herne, have requested the favour of this interview for the purpose of offering to you an expression of our profound respect and deep gratitude.

Sojourners in your land and separated from the many dear ties of our Fatherland, strangers amid strangers, but for you we had been spiritually displaced, no minister of our Religion who could speak our language resided near us and we were thus deprived of the great blessing and consolation consigned in our Holy Church, till it pleased God to bring you to our aid.

You, Reverend Sir, not bound to us by ties of country or ecclesiastical duty, influenced alone by the pure spirit of a Christian minister, you heard of our isolation and spiritual wants and declared yourself willing to relieve these wants, and in imitation of your great Master, you invited all to come to you, and find consolation and peace. You spoke the words of eternal love to us, in our own language and sought to cast off the burden of Sin from our souls, according to us the saving sacraments of our Church. But beyond all this you have been a Benefactor to us, for when you learned that in consequence of the distance of the Collieries from Düsseldorf very many of the workmen and their families were unable to go to you, you offered to come to us, declining to permit us to defray your travelling expenses. You have fulfilled your promise, in spite of your present ill health, forgetful of your suffering and weakened strength, listening only to the voice of God, you came to instruct, admonish and comfort our wives, our families, and ourselves. For all this we beg to offer our fervent thanks, our deep respect and our heartfelt gratitude. We are also, Reverend Sir, assembled around you today in order to pray your acceptance of the accompanying chalice, hoping it may sometimes help to recall to your mind the humble Irish workmen, in whose hearts your generous goodness shall ever remain faithfully recorded, and we trust that the sacred purposes which belong to our offering, may give it a value in your eyes. In conclusion, we would add our anxious entreaty that when you minister at God's Holy Altar there may at times arrive from your lips to the Throne of God, application for us that your effort on our behalf may not through our unworthiness prove unavailable.

Accept, Reverend Sir, our earnest prayers that Almighty God may restore you to health and spare you yet longer for the fulfilment of your high and sacred duties.

Signed by:
Michael McGurrin, George Doran, Frances Corr, Edward Bradley, Bernard Hatten, Thomas Hogan, Charles Hatten, William Murphy, James Keenan, Bernard Hone, John Bready, William Keating, James McDonnell, Patrick Ward, John McGurrin, John Purcell, Thomas McGreven, Francis Deignan, James Lacy, Bernard McDonnell, James Arthur.

Appendix III

The Irish Sea Cross-Channel Sailings 1860–1872

To illustrate Mulvany's attention to detail in the preparation of his numerous memoranda (27 in all) an excerpt from one entitled 'Projected International Traffic in Northern and Eastern Europe via the New Harbour in Flushing', Düsseldorf, September 1873, is included which analyses the performances of four 2,000-ton steamers plying between Kingstown and Holyhead during the twelve years from 1860 to 1872.

With allowance for delays due to bad weather and fog, the four vessels in that period made 17,528 crossings with an average duration of 3 hours 55 minutes for the 65.5 English miles distance.

It is not a little surprising that many years later the sailing time on this route for ferry steamers has been only slightly reduced!

Connaught		Leinster		Munster		Ulster	
Trips	Time	Trips	Time	Trips	Time	Trips	Time
2606	3h55m	1970	3h56m	2000	3h59m	2169	4h1m
2163	3h51m	2323	3h51m	2180	3h52m	2117	3h55m

The first row is for winter sailings (6 months), the second is for summer sailings – annual figures.

Appendix IV

Share Transfers

Extracts from Minutes of Board Meetings of Hibernia and Shamrock (Source: Archives of Bochum Mining Museum).

25-11-1854 Michael Corr van der Maeren, W. T. Mulvany and James Perry bought 85 kuxen in 'Ludwigsglück' from Samuel Ryland Phipson, financial agent, Brussels. Price: 6,821 thaler.

19-04-1855 Corr van der Maeren sold 12 kuxen to Joseph Malcolmson.
Price: 200 thaler or £6,480.

25-03-1856 Corr van der Maeren and W. T. Mulvany held 80 kuxen. Sold 24 kuxen to other members of board.

26-03-1856 W. T. Mulvany sold 16 kuxen to Joseph Malcolmson. Price: 6,400 thaler.

13-10-1857 Michael Corr van der Maeren gave 1 kuxe to sister Hélène Couvreur, wife of August Peter Couvreur, editor, *Independence Belge*, Brussels (wedding present).

08-10-1860 W. T. Mulvany transferred 2 kuxen each to Alicia Anne (wife) and Annabella Catherine (daughter).

17-01-1866 W. T. Mulvany sold 2 kuxen in Hibernia to John Latimer, a nephew in Board of Works.
Price: £1,000.

27-02-1872 W. R. Mulvany gave his daughter, Mary Seebohm, 1 kuxe (wedding present).

Note: The value of a kuxe varied greatly between £650 and £1,000, sometimes even more.

Appendix V

List of Memoranda written by William Thomas Mulvany during his residence in Düsseldorf 1856–1885

1. Memorandum on the 'Pfennig a Mile' Tariff – Stuttgart, 8 May 1860.
2. 'Germany's Progress in the Coal and Iron Industries and her Dependence upon the Railways' – Düsseldorf, 8 May 1868.
3. 'Germany's Coal and Coal Exports, Part I, Holland' – Düsseldorf 1869.
4. 'Practical Suggestions for the Solution to the Transport Emergency' Düsseldorf 1872.
   'The Miners' Strike in the Essen Region. A Few Friendly Words to the Employers and the Workers' – Düsseldorf, 21 June 1872.
6. 'Projected International Traffic in Northern and Eastern Europe via the New Harbour in Flushing' – Düsseldorf, September 1873.
   'Germany's Railway Tariff' – Düsseldorf, January 1874.
   'For and Against the Tariff Increase' – Düsseldorf, 30 April 1874.
9. 'Memorandum on the Results of the Railway Tariff Increase' – Düsseldorf, 20 December 1874.
10. 'Germany's North Sea Harbours and their Railway Connections' – W. T. Mulvany and H. Haniel, Düsseldorf and Ruhrort, 27 December 1874.
    'Westphalian Coal Export Committee' – Düsseldorf, 23 September 1876.
12. 'Germany's Trade Policy and its Effect on the National Welfare' – Düsseldorf, 30 November 1876.
13. 'Germany's Traffic Affairs' – Düsseldorf, January 1877.
    'Memorandum on the Reform of Railway Freight Tariffs' – Düsseldorf, July 1879.
    'The Facilities of a Central Railway Station etc. with Regard to International Traffic and Connection to the Rhine' – Düsseldorf 1880.
    'Germany's Waterways and Improvements in Shipbuilding' – Berlin, 12 January 1881.
17. 'Germany's Waterways II' – Düsseldorf, 12 May 1881.

18. 'Germany's Waterways III' – 21 May 1881
19. 'Germany's Waterways IV' – Düsseldorf, 15 June 1881.
    'The Inland Shipping System, Improvement of the Belgian Inland Traffic' – Düsseldorf, 26 December 1881.
21. 'Düsseldorf's Railway and Harbour Questions' – Düsseldorf, 10 February 1882.
    'The Düsseldorf Harbour Question' – Düsseldorf 1875, 1884 and by Thomas Robert Mulvany, Düsseldorf, 28 June 1889.
    'Amalgamation of Coal-Mines in a Part of the Dortmund Region' – W. T. and T. R. Mulvany, Düsseldorf, 10 October 1882.
24. 'River-Sea Steamships' – Düsseldorf, 7 January 1884.
    'Memorandum on the Dual Currency' – Düsseldorf, 18 August 1885.
26. 'The Currency Question. Depression in Trade and Transport' – Düsseldorf, September 1885.
27. 'The Currency Question. Memorandum for Delegate Meeting of the Central Association of German Industrialists in Köln', October 1885.

Memoranda written in Ireland

'Abstract of Observations on Regulating Weirs' (Inst. of Civil Engineers of Ireland), Vol. 1, 1843, Wm. T. Mulvany.
'On the Drainage and Improvement of Ballyteigue Lough' (Inst. of Civil Engineers of Ireland), Trans. Vol. 1, 1845, Wm. T. Mulvany.
'On Several Collections of Antiquities Made by the Officers of the Board Works and Presented to the Academy (RHA)', Vol. V (1850–1953). Wm. T. Mulvany.
'On Facts Connected with the Art of Blasting Operations', Trans. Vol. IV, 1851, Wm. T. Mulvany.
'On the Use of Screw Pumps for Unwatering Works' (Inst. of Civil Engineers of Ireland), 1851 by Thomas James Mulvany.

Appendix VI

International Communication in the North and East of Europe through the New Harbour of Flushing at the Mouth of the Scheldt in Holland

by
Wm. T. Mulvany
Formerly Commissioner of Public Works, Ireland,
President of the Council of the Prussian Mining and Iron Work Company Düsseldorf

Printed for Private Circulation

Düsseldorf, September 1873
Printed by Spiethoff & Krahe
Transcript from original

To obtain the maximum of advantages and the utmost speed consistent with safety in the personal and postal communications between Nations – according to the circumstances of each case – Railways – by land – and deep Harbours, accessible at all times for the most powerful Steamers – by water – both in the nearest practical direct route, constitute plainly the first essentials of success.

Railways
The great mission of Railways will, however, not be fulfilled until they are made perfect, in design, construction and use.

Even now we see how completely all old world maxims – theories and experiences in great political – war – and commercial questions, are altered or nullified by the progress and extension of railways and improved modes of communication, especially when not confined to any one country, but extending over the boundaries of several countries, constituting, by degrees, a net-work over vast continents, and, combined with Steam Navigation, over the world.

Mankind is surprised at the results in wars, at the sudden great influx and reflux of money and the other rapidly occurring crises in money matters – the sudden flood of prosperity following the establishment of peace – and last not least the rapid spread of enlarged and sounder views on religion and education (everywhere outside those walls where men wilfully seclude themselves and shut out the light and experience of the world's progress); but the moving and immediate mechanical causes – Steam and Electricity, Railways, Steam-Ships and the Telegraph – with their daily accumulative results on the whole life and business of man, must be palpably plain to all calm reflecting minds.

The Nations which have not yet obtained the advantage of these mechanical means of all progress cannot longer hold their place without them; unknown countries, deserts and wilds must be slowly but surely opened up and rendered available for mankind and civilisation by importing these invincible conquerors, these, in reality, most suitable though slow means of secure discovery and development; and we cannot doubt that ere long the very heart of Africa, which has so long been hidden from civilised man – and which, lying so near Europe and Asia, still shows on the map of the world – a void blank – if not disgraceful to the civilised nations of the world, at least challenging their enterprise and manhood to fulfil the first command of the Creator, will be traversed and made accessible to civilisation.

But if it be a want or a duty to extend these benefits to countries which have not hitherto enjoyed them, how much more is it essential for the Governments of old countries to make their systems of communication perfect and adequate not merely to their present wants (as was the economic rule in old times, 'to let the necessity or want beget the improvement') but also for those rapidly and surely coming increased wants which it is the peculiar feature of these improved systems themselves to beget.

The traffic consequent upon, or as we may say actually created by, railways far exceeds that which ever existed or could be calculated upon before their construction – and within reasonable limits this may fairly be contemplated to be the consequence of new lines.

The old railway nations of Europe if they will maintain their status and the superiority which they have hitherto obtained by their works, must go on, improve and complete their systems of communication, and each is especially bound in its own interest to do so in connection with the progress of its neighbour.

In this great question of communication little or no attention appears to have been given to any general or international plan – each country has adopted its own plan – or perhaps more properly said – no plan. For if one examines the railway maps of Europe there is even in each separate country little evidence as yet of a carefully – previously devised – general plan of which each line, as constructed, was to form a part; with the exception of France where centralisation and radiation from Paris (on the principle that Paris was France) as a centre forms a clear and prominent feature of a previously devised plan.

In England, as is well known, no general plan, not even a general railway law made – railways were initiated by joint-stock companies as each thought most advantageous, and rectification of plan took place subsequently under the pressure of a stimulating competition between great numbers of companies.

In Belgium, there is no other evidence of a plan up to any recent date except a general net, as it were, by which towns are connected with each other.

From Germany, taken as a whole, with its numerous states and their separate systems, and even from Prussia, separated as it was in different parts by intervening small independent states, it was not to be expected that much uniformity or singleness of plan could be carried out – and this is sufficiently evident in the result.

Still in Prussia, notwithstanding its mixed system of state railways, private railways managed by private companies and private railways managed by the state; there is still evidence of the perpetual struggle, as it were, which the government has, under such disadvantages, been making to carry out a plan upon given principles – of which of late the main object seems to be to maintain the mixed system and to counteract the effect of some of the evils which arise perhaps inevitably from investing the monopolies of public highways of communication in private interested joint-stock companies, and once recognised and established by granting to them large and extended lines and districts – thereby producing 'ab initio' the position which the joint-stock companies of England are now seeking to obtain by amalgamation.

I will not here discuss the vexed question whether the granting of Public railways to private companies is right or wrong – I propose to deal for practical purposes with the facts as they are.

But whatever system is to continue I submit that it is now full time when the whole of Germany is united into one Empire, that the organisation of its means of communication and especially of its railways into a uniform or a 'planmässiges' system, and making them as perfect both in administration of the present and the designing, laying out and construction of new lines as it is practically possible to do, should be undertaken as not only expected by the world from the genius of German statesmen and the talent of their engineers, but as essential – perhaps I may be allowed to say – in the first degree – to the future industrial and commercial interests of the Empire and to those great international lines of communication which must naturally, by its central geographical position, take their course through Germany.

Similar observations are clearly applicable to Holland and Belgium which will enjoy in the highest degree the first and accumulated fruits of the international communication to which this paper refers; and to Russia, Austria, Hungary and Turkey to the quick development of whose best interests in every respect the completion of the improved communication here contemplated would be of vital importance.

The wants of civilisation and of the world demand in this age the shortest and quickest and therefore the straightest and best lines of communication, 'the crooked ways must be made straight' and all experience in Railway construction tends to the abandonment of circuitous routes for direct. For through-going traffic and postal communications between distant countries these principles are becoming daily more essential and all the improvements hitherto obtained over the slow coaching of old times only renders us more sensibly alive to the absence of that perfection in the present lines of communication of which they are palpably capable.

Notwithstanding the very great improvements made in the present year, the time occupied, for example, even with express trains between, say, Berlin and London for passengers and letters at the shortest 30 hours and between Düsseldorf and London 22 hours, (whilst the shortest between London and Düsseldorf is 16 hours) is far too long, and can, as hereinafter shown be most materially reduced.

It would be, however, to imitate the folly of the Ostrich if we shut our eyes and ears to the statistics of Railways, or hesitate for these international lines at least (if not for all passenger and postal lines) to decide that they shall be constructed and worked wherever new lines are required – or shall be altered in construction and worked wherever existing lines can be adopted into the system on principles by which the mission of Railways can be truly and perfectly fulfilled.

I do not expect that any experienced Railway Practitioner or authority will contend that this cannot be done but many will exclaim against the additional cost or expense of construction.

If it can be done then I contend it is the duty of the Governments and Legislations of Europe (at least) as the birth-place of Railways to insist that it should be done.

As regards the additional cost of construction I presume to say I have seen, as yet, no place in Europe where for such purposes as are here contemplated, (if the funds be truly devoted under judicious management to work and not wasted in preliminaries as in some countries or in Share and Exchange speculations as in others) the necessary works for a perfect system of Railway cannot be executed with results commensurate, on the whole, to the expenditure, and I would remark that the first cost of a perfect system however apparently high – when confined to useful, not ornamental work – rarely fails to be remunerative, from the greater economy in the working for the long ages the Railway has to endure.

I premise the above as I anticipate there will be still found some to oppose or at least to express alarm at the extent to which I would propose to go to make these international Railways as complete and perfect as it appears to me they should be for such a purpose.

For these international lines and especially for the main trunks of the system – the Railways should pass over or under every other line of communication. No level crossings of Railways, Roads, Navigations or even footpaths should be allowed. – The Railways should be constructed with double line in the centre for all passenger and postal trains – the passengers traffic separated from the goods and mineral traffic, especially at all stations; arrival and departure platforms and buildings provided at such stations, no facing points allowed on the passenger lines under any circumstances, not head stations except at termini, and then constructed with abundant length beyond the arrival platform, and in short the whole construction should be adapted for running express trains at the highest attainable speed without risk of collision, with sleeping carriages and all the means of living in the trains themselves for the long journeys which under such circumstances and with such improved accommodation would be then freely undertaken by thousands who at present prefer to remain at home.

International lines to be so worked should for the greater part be designed for 4 lines of Rails and in their earth and masonry works constructed, therefore, though of course the two additional lines would only be laid down when necessary; but there is little doubt that in a very few years a great through traffic for long distances in goods, cattle, etc. would arise which would render these additional lines necessary and remunerative.

In the mean time the existing crooked and cross lines of Railway of the country which would not admit of adaptation into the international system would be abundantly occupied in the local passenger, goods and mineral traffic of the country and at important fixed stations joins into the international lines for the transfer of passengers, post and goods.

On the principles above enumerated many great and important international lines of communication can and doubtless soon will be devised for passing through Europe in various directions. My residence here in the Rhine Province for 18 years and my personal experience of the want of improved communication has naturally turned my attention to the north of Europe – the connection of the steam Navigation of the Atlantic through the natural entrepot of the English Channel to the East of Europe and the often mooted question of the best line of communication between England and India, and I wish to illustrate the views I have long entertained on the subjects by the sketch of a project for international communication through the new harbour of Flushing described in this paper and delineated roughly on the annexed Map.

Harbours
The first consideration was to determine on the Harbour which would be most suitable for the terminus of the International Railway and at various times I visited and inspected all the Harbours along the North Sea from Boulogne to the Elbe with the exception of the Helder and Harlingen, the positions of which rendered them of comparatively little interest to the object which I had in view in my tours.

The investigation of these various Harbours is full of interest to the engineer showing along this long stretch of low coast with its peculiar delta formation the great efforts which different nations have made to contend with nature and overcome difficulties of no ordinary kind. At the same time it opens a great field for the exercise of the talents of the engineer who carefully studies the delta forming Rivers and Estuaries where they exist, and who avails himself judiciously of the forces of nature in the flood and ebb of the sea and the discharge of Rivers to carry out plans in aid of nature for the improvement of Harbours and the attainment of deep channels of access to them at all times of the tide.[1]

This is not the place to discuss such questions or to enter into a detailed description of all these Harbours. It will perhaps be sufficient for the purpose of this paper to say that the Roadstead of Flush-

---

1 *Emden is a case in point having great natural capabilities, requiring no doubt considerable expenditure, but promising great success as an efficient Harbour for a large District and back country requiring such a Harbour and a great maritime trade.*

ing has ever had by nature deep water at all times of tide and is rarely, if ever, incommoded by ice; whilst the Harbours to the west, including Calais and Ostend – notwithstanding the most judicious and effective works of art there constructed, offer by nature little if any hope of ever having deep water; and the Harbours to the East are either bar Harbours, not accessible at all times of tide – as Rotterdam – or are impeded by ice in winter and for the most part lie, as will be seen by the Map, too far East to suit the line of international communication under consideration.

For my part therefore, after careful study of the Harbour and the marine charts, I saw years ago that if Flushing Harbour were properly improved, or rather a Harbour and Dock constructed and properly connected with its own deep water roadstead, and connected by Railway with the Continental net of Railways, it was by Nature, by its projecting position into the sea, and would by necessity be the great Harbour and entrepot of the future international communication for this part of Europe.

Holland has during the last 10 or 12 years made, steadily and quietly, immense progress in her Public Works executed by the state directly, in her system of State Railways and great Bridges constructed under very difficult circumstances – in her large Harbour at Rotterdam and the 'Hook of Holland' – in this very extensive work of the new Harbour, Docks and Canal at Flushing and in aiding the construction of the new Harbour and Canal at Amsterdam, all works of considerable Engineering difficulty and all so far successfully carried out or progressing to completion – all taken together affording a very brilliant example of how much a State can accomplish in that class of Public Works which is the proper object for State expenditure when this expenditure is judiciously laid out and properly controlled.

I have very recently seen the works at Flushing; the conditions which were previously wanted are now fulfilled. It is connected by Railway with the whole Continental system – admirable and capacious deep water Docks are erected and an outer Harbour connecting it with the deep water of the Roadstead – all fully adequate for the commercial wants of the port at present, and for some years to come, and only deficient in one point (which however can be easily remedied) for the great purpose of the termina Harbour of International Communication for which I consider its position so peculiarly fits it.

The point to which I refer is the size of the outer Harbour into which, according to the project, the large and powerful Passenger and

Mail Steamers to and from the Atlantic, and those required for very high speed to and from England should be enabled to come at all times of tide, day and night, without difficulty or delay – deliver their Passengers and Mails direct off their decks into the Railway carriages on an ample pier in the centre of the Harbour, and then warping round to the departure platform at the other side of the pier, or one side of the Harbour as the case might be, hold themselves prepared to leave the Harbour when necessary. For such purposes the outer Harbour is quite too small and even the entrance rather too confined. In the annexed plan I have sketched the least dimension to which the outer Harbour should be extended for this purpose, and shown the central arrival and departure pier for the large Steamers designed on the principle which has proved eminently successful in the Harbour of Kingstown constructed for the arrival and departure of the Mail Steamers between England and Ireland.

Fortunately, there is little difficulty in thus extending the outer Harbour at Flushing and I take the liberty of thus early making the suggestion – as at least so far useful that it may lead to the reservation on the part of the Government of Holland of all adjacent lands which may be required for the future extension and improvement of this important Port. Nature has done everything for the Roadstead to entitle it to be selected as the great terminus for this international communication, but to fulfil its mission the artificial works must be so constructed so as to admit the largest Atlantic Mail Steamers as above described.

The Project
For international communication which I take the liberty to submit for the consideration of all interested and as illustrative of the principles set forth in this paper is as follows:

The terminal Harbour being thus fixed it becomes next of importance to decide upon the direction of the first part of the Main Trunk line which shall best suit the diverging branches of the systems it is intended to serve.

Venlo on the frontier between Holland and Germany is, by its geographical position as well as by the existing great lines of Railway, clearly indicated as the best common or medium point from which a proposed international system of communication with Flushing for its terminal Harbour should diverge.

Venlo is, for instance, very little to the south of a direct line from Flushing to Berlin, through which will naturally pass the traffic to St Petersburg; and very little to the north of a direct line from

Flushing to Vienna, through which will naturally pass the traffic to Constantinople, whilst it joins the lines from the capitals of France and Belgium to the North and East of Europe.

Finally, Venlo is at present connected not only with Flushing Harbour but is also connected, or in course of being so, with all the great routes contemplated in this project by Railways which it is proposed in many cases to utilise or adopt for the present with the alterations proposed in the first part of this paper; and in some others (when the existing lines are more suitable by their construction for local traffic) to replace from time to time by more direct and more suitably constructed lines.

Thus then, without much delay after the opening of the Harbour of Flushing by suitable international organisation, a considerable improvement, in the transmission of Passengers and Mails between the East and West of Europe might be effected; but to attain the speed required and to make the systems complete – to make it worthy of the great objects and the great nations whose interests are involved – it will, at the very least, be necessary to carry out the works and effect the objects described in this paper.

England, the English Channel and Flushing

Assuming the outer, or entrance Harbour of Flushing to be extended as proposed to fit it for the reception of the powerful Steamers referred to, then I have no doubt that the Mail and Passenger traffic between, say, London and Flushing can be effected within 6 hours.

The Harbours of Dover and Harwich are now available for such a communication, whilst I have little doubt, as an engineer, that the time will come when by suitable works Margate can be made available for this purpose. Sheerness, Queensborough, and other points of departure within the Thames, afford ample facilities through their Railway connections for Passenger traffic and will no doubt be made available.

The following are the distances from Flushing, to

Ramsgate	20 miles
Margate	21 miles
Dover	22 miles
Harwich	24 miles
London	36 miles

The mile is 7,407 metres.

One of the great advantages to Holland and Belgium and all the Nations to the east of them is that all the Passengers and Mails destined for these countries from all parts of the world which come by sea through the English Channel can be landed here and transmitted to their destinations with the least possible delay – and of course equal facilities afforded to the outgoing Passengers and Mail.

Flushing to Venlo
The newly completed Railway from Flushing through the Islands of Walcheren and South Beveland to the main land near Bergen-op-Zoom is in the right direction and can easily be increased in its dimensions and fitted with 4 lines of rails to suit the great main trunk line of this international system – but from Woensdrecht on the main land where the line turns to the north to Bergen-op-Zoom the circuitous routes of the Railway to Venlo and the local character of their construction will, in my opinion, call for the construction of a new, straight, main trunk line between Woensdrecht and Venlo with a short junction to Antwerp and thereby a direct connection to Ghent and Ostend on the one hand and to Brussels and Calais on the other.

This straight line will pass chiefly through Holland and for a short distance through Belgium, the commercial interests of both which countries will be so materially promoted, by having the Scheldt used as the great entrepot of this part of Europe, that there can be no doubt entertained of their Governments agreeing to perfect this part of the proposed international communication.

It is unnecessary, here, to enter into detail as to all the Passenger and Postal arrangements which can be arranged for Holland and Belgium by the establishment of this communication between Flushing and Venlo; they will be self-evident to every observant person.

Venlo to Bremen, Hamburg and Denmark
From Venlo the newly constructed almost direct line by Wesel on the Rhine, Münster, Osnabrück, Bremen and Hamburg approaches completion and when regulated as above proposed for the reception of international traffic by the removal of all level crossings or other impediments to the safe working of express trains will form the most suitable northern branch of this international system to Hamburg and Denmark and all the intervening and adjacent countries.

The enormous advantages of saving of time for passengers and mails by the adoption of this route and the express system proposed, requires, at least for the parties interested and resident in the cities and town along it, no comment.

Venlo to Berlin and St Petersburg

From Venlo to the Rhine and Dortmund in the direction to Berlin, and from Venlo to the Rhine at Düsseldorf there exist a great number of Railway lines, made by various parties – for various objects – but without any great or national plan in view and by a strange fatality scarcely any of them suitable for the great international and express traffic contemplated in this paper.

In the great mineral district between the Rhine and Dortmund, it is true, express trains have been recently, and are now daily, running through all the coal trains and miserably insufficient stations, level crossings of railways and roads over railways suitable, now at least, only for local traffic – but this is a risk of such magnitude as nothing but the most absolute necessity and the want of a suitable line for this express traffic, can justify.

Fortunately, the German Government have recently, as I understand, decided upon a most suitable site for a Bridge over the Rhine, up stream from Ruhrort and between that town and Duisburg; and doubtless the Government will, with a view to the great international traffic, arrange that this bridge shall be constructed to carry, at least, 4 lines of rails and to suit the wants of the coming future as well as the present.

For the great international traffic to Berlin, St Petersburgh (sic) and the North-East of Europe I submit that no petty difficulties or narrow and mistaken views of economy should stand in the way of the construction of the most direct and most perfect Railway which can be constructed, and that in devising such a line the wants of the future, the enormous increased traffic which that future will certainly develope (sic), should be fully weighed and considered.

My study of the country for some years in furtherance of this view leads me to propose a straight line from Venlo to the proposed bridge between Ruhrort and Duisburg thence, in the straight direction, through the middle of the Westphalian coal district between Essen and the laine of the Emsher valley a little to the north of Dortmund and a little to the south of Hamm direct through the valley of the Lippe and in the best practicable line through or near Detmold near Hanover to Lehrte from which the Lehrte-Stendal line with the necessary modifications can be adopted to Berlin.

From Berlin the best existing direct Railway route suited for express trains will be adopted to St Petersburg and the traffic to the many important intermediate places easily arranged according to the peculiar circumstances of each.

Venlo, Düsseldorf, Elberfeld to Middle Germany and Russia
Although lines exist from Venlo to Düsseldorf which suit the present traffic, yet, I have been long convinced that for the purposes here contemplated a direct line from Venlo to Düsseldorf crossing the Rhine on the down stream side of the town combined with a very ample harbour there, will become an absolute necessity for the greatly increasing manufactures of the district between Venlo and Hagen.

Such a line will in my opinion be not only necessary for the branch to Middle Germany – but even still more for the completion of the most direct line to Vienna and Constantinople hereinafter referred to.

From Düsseldorf the Bergisch-Märkisch system with considerable alterations or a greatly improved line can be used to Hagen and thence the Ruhrthalbahn and other existing railways would form the branch under consideration, but with many important ameliorations, to Cassel, Halle, Leipsic (*sic*), Dresden, Breslau, Warsaw and ultimately, no doubt, to Moscow – serving at all these stations for the East and West traffic of the great district connected with these cities by existing railways.

Venlo to South Germany and Switzerland
The Rhenish railway on the left bank of the Rhine, and which is at present connected with Venlo, will naturally take up this traffic and, with the other existing railways maintain the express communication with the capital towns of South Germany, Carlsruhe, Stutgart (*sic*) and Munich and with Switzerland.

The Rhenish and Hessian Ludwigsbahn by Darmstadt to Aschaffenburg will with the Bavarian railways, as at present, serve for a considerable time for the express traffic between Venlo, Vienna and the East; but it is scarcely necessary for me to repeat that to fully adopt these existing railways for the express traffic for passengers and mails contemplated in this project many important alterations and improvements, of the nature referred to in the first part of this paper, will be indispensable.

Venlo, Vienna to Constantinople, England to India
Inferior perhaps to none of the branches of this project in importance to Europe and Asia, or at least to the nations of both Continents immediately concerned, is the great line of international communication designated by this title.

All authorities who have contemplated a Railway communication between India and England have, almost of necessity, regarded Constantinople as a fixed point in the line; and it will be readily seen that Vienna, which lies nearly in the direct line between Venlo and Constantinople, becomes, even independently of other great considerations, geographically another fixed point in this part of our project.

I have stated above that for the present the traffic can be carried on by the existing route, Venlo to Mainz, Darmstadt, Nurenburg (sic), Passau, Linz to Vienna but even if we measure the importance of this line by considerations limited to the passenger and mail traffic of Austria, Hungary, Roumania and Turkey to Constantinople irrespective of the more distant prospects of communication with Persia and India by the Euphrates valley – it is clear and incontestable that the most perfectly devised trunk line should be constructed in the most direct line which the country will admit of, between Venlo and Vienna whereby a great saving in distance and time would be effected.

Such a direct line would pass from Venlo direct to Düsseldorf as already proposed and thence to Siegen, and so far I have reason to believe it is practicable and required even at present by the local wants of the district. How the straightest line can be practically made from thence to Vienna I cannot say as I have never examined the country, but the main points in the straight line judging from the map are Fulda, Beuruth (sic) and Budweis to Vienna, and there can be little doubt that a suitable line, much nearer to the straight direction than Bingen and Darmstadt can be found.

From Vienna the existing line to Pesth and thence to Piski and Petroseney in the Carpathian Mountains near the borders of Roumania I can, from my own inspection in the present summer, speak of as being suitable or easy to be made suitable for the extension in the desired direction of this international system.

From Pesth to Constantinople or into Roumania, another line might be selected, as for example by Czegled, Szegeden, to Temesvar and thence by the existing line to the Danube at Baziash, from which place I understand a line has been projected to Constantinople; or from Temesvar by a line already projected and which must for the Mineral and Agricultural interests of this rich district be constructed along the valley of the Temes to Karansebes and then by Mahadia near the famous and delightfully situated Hercules Baths to the Danube at Orasova, from whence by the 'Iron door' it could proceed through Roumania either to Varna or possibly more direct to Constantinople.

But I prefer the line by Petroseney because it is more direct and the line is already constructed and open to Petroseney; where at a height of 2,000 feet above the sea, it enters a stone coal district with existing collieries, worked by the Kronstädter Verein and the Hungarian Government (who have both established excellent colonies of workmen) and an almost inexhaustible supply of admirable locomotive and manufacturing coal exists, of which I satisfied myself by personal inspection of the collieries in June last.

Such a supply of coal, on the direct line of Railway, and in a country where some of the richest and purest iron ores I have almost ever seen, exist in abundance, and are being already worked in blast furnaces erected by the Kronstädter Verein at Kalan (where the best Bessemer steel rails can be produced), would be of almost incalculable value to Roumania and Turkey if this line were carried through instead of stopping as at present at Petroseney.

Fortunately, even in this great Mountain District, the little river the Shill, which takes its rise in the coal valley referred to, breaks directly opposite Petroseney, through the mountain range, in a grand chasm, with a regular fall into the plains of Roumania, close to the so called Vulcan Pass, and though eliciting all the energy and talent of the engineer (perhaps by the adoption of a combination of short tunnels and side cuttings in rock) presenting in these days of engineering skill, no great difficulty for the construction of this most important line of Railway.

Anticipated Results

With the deep water Harbour of Flushing completed, and connected by rail with the main land – and assuming that the simple principles of Railway construction, improvement, and adaptation to the necessities of safe and quick transit referred to in this paper, will be adopted, so as to make these lines examples to the world – let us see by a few cases what would be the effect on the Passenger and Postal traffic over these international lines if properly organised and carried out.

Assuming only the rate of speed at present attained by express trains in Germany, and express Steamers between England and Ireland, I venture to assert that Passengers and Mails can be carried from

London to Hamburg in 16 hours
do. to Berlin, Dresden, Munich in 18 hours
do. to Düsseldorf, Elberfeld, Cologne 10 to 11 hours

do. to Vienna in 24 hours
do. to St Petersburgh and Constantinople in 48 hours
and, of course, on the return journeys in the same time.

I think we may also safely anticipate, that for such a traffic, through-going trains and suitable sleeping and living carriages will be constructed and used – that from and to the post, the passenger will be made fully as comfortable as in his own house – that the inconveniences of Customs' investigations on the frontiers will be completely avoided by suitable arrangements at the starting and arrival stations, and that in a word the true mission of Railways as the most perfect, rapid and safe mode of transit, will before long be fulfilled.

If this assumption be right what will be the result?

Let the most cautious and foreseeing thinkers answer!

I conclude with the simple expression of the hope, that the debt of gratitude, which the practical West, owes to the classical East, from which we received so much in the past, will be repaid with usury, by the revival of a civilisation, a religion, a morality and a material prosperity which our iron ways, our intimate union, and daily intercourse, appears perhaps best calculated to promote.

Pempelfort, Düsseldorf, 1 September 1873
Stamped: Wm. T. Mulvany

Appendix VII

Notes on the Principal Investors
The Malcolmson Brothers and Henry Bewley

Even by present-day standards, the investment proposal, which W. T. Mulvany put before several wealthy merchant princes in Ireland, was a very long shot. Up to then there was very little experience of coal-mining in Ireland and the idea of developing and operating a mine in a foreign environment was, as far as the main potential investors were concerned, without precedent. For the Perrys, the Malcolmsons and later Henry Bewley and the Goodbodys, as well as the Mulvanys themselves, this was a risky venture capital project.

The principal investors in the first Hibernia coal-mine in Gelsenkirchen were the Malcolmson family of Waterford. Originally of Scottish origin, their forebears had settled in Ireland in the seventeenth century and were weavers in the linen industry in Lurgan. In 1748, Joseph Malcolmson married into a Quaker family and he and his wife, Rachel, had eleven children. Two of these children, John and David, moved to Clonmel and established flour mills there and in Pouldrew and Carrick-on-Suir. In the year 1826, a quarter of all flour exported from the port of Waterford emanated from the Malcolmson mills.

At the same time, David Malcolmson set up a cotton mill at Portlaw. He built a canal linking the River Clodagh with the River Suir to allow barges to ply between his mill and Waterford Port. There is evidence in the annals of this wealthy family to suggest that enterprise, innovation and prudent risk-taking were inherited attributes. David died in 1844 at the age of 79. By now the family was involved in flour-milling, cotton-milling (the raw cotton was imported from the southern states of North America), railways, fisheries, peat works and shipping. A substantial shareholding in the P & O Shipping Company was part of the investment portfolio. David's eldest son, Joseph, became manager of the company.

Under Joseph's management, the business expaned. At this time the city of Waterford had earned an enviable reputation for shipbuilding and repair and it was the main industry in the city. There were four shipyards on the River Suir building a wide range of vessels both in wood and steel. Perhaps it was the involvement with the P & O Line that stimulated Joseph Malcolmson in 1843 (a year before his father died) to set up the Neptune Ironworks on the banks of the river. This new yard achieved a reputation for well-designed and well-built vessels. At first these were smaller ships intended for either cross-channel or the European trade, but as the company's status grew orders were received from the continent and as far away as the Ukraine. Between 1847 and 1882, forty vessels were built at Malcolmson's yard in Waterford. Some of these were up to 4,000 tons displacement.

When W. T. Mulvany approached Joseph Malcolmson with the proposal of participating in what eventually became the Hibernia colliery in the Ruhr it is likely that the idea met with an immediate response. The real possibility, later to become a reality, of obtaining bunkers for his own vessels from his own coal-mine was most desirable for the astute entrepreneur. The diversity of the family's commercial activities at this time indicates a capability and willingness to expand in many directions.

It is not on record how many workers in total were employed in the Malcolmson operations but at least 400 were employed in the Neptune Ironworks. The first vessel of 326 tons, the *Neptune*, was built in 1847 and when Joseph Malcolmson founded the St Petersburg Steamship Company, this vessel opened the first regular service between London and the Russian port. On her first voyage, she took on board the mayor of St Petersburg at Kronstadt and sailed up to the harbour on the Neva where all ships were dressed with bunting. Czar Nicholas I, aboard his state barge, was on hand to greet the *Neptune* and to mark the occasion he ordered that the vessel be freed of pilot and harbour dues on all her subsequent visits.

The change-over from paddle to screw propulsion was taking place at this time and the Neptune yard was foremost in promoting this innovation. Comparative studies were undertaken and Joseph Malcolmson persuaded his fellow-shareholders on the P & O board to follow this new trend.

The American Civil War (1861–1865) interfered with the importation of raw cotton to Waterford, affecting the mills in Clonmel and Carrick-on-Suir. Between 1861 and 1866 the Malcolmson family built large houses in Dunmore East (now the Haven Hotel), in Portlaw (Clodogh, Elva and Woodlock), and one in Clonmel (Minella). William Malcolmson is said to have invested substantial capital in various doubtful enterprises. In 1858, Joseph Malcolmson's widow withdrew her shareholding as did his aunt Rachel. With the slump in the cotton trade, the core operation, the viability of the family business was not endangered but the departure of these two family members threw a shadow on the fortunes of the company.

In 1867 Joseph's eldest son, David died of 'intemperance' at the relatively young age of 37 and his widow, through the courts, took her share of £198,000 out of the business and the family bankers, Overund & Gurney in London filed for bankruptcy with losses of £13 million. Much of this money belonged to the Waterford family. Inevitably, the Malcolmson enterprise went bankrupt in 1877. However, the Neptune yard completed orders already on the stocks and the last vessel, a steam-yacht named *Maritana*, was launched in 1882. The company was later taken over by the Limerick Steamship Company.

For the Malcolmsons the venture capital investment in the Ruhr coal-mines with the Mulvanys was just another part of their large portfolio as was also the case with the Perrys and the Goodbodys. In the initial twelve years of the project in Prussia, good dividends were earned and the family was content to leave the technical and commercial management entirely in Mulvany's hands.

Unfortunately, the downturn in the Malcolmson fortunes coincided with the first crises in the coal industry in the Ruhr and the first disagreement with Mulvany which eventually led to the sale of the collieries to the Berliner Handelsbank.

Henry Bewley
Henry Bewley, of Willow Park, Dublin, 1804–1876, was one of eleven children. The Bewleys were Quakers. His father, Samuel, was a leading personality in Dublin's commercial circles, being a shipowner and treasurer of the Dublin Chamber of Commerce. He founded the National Assurance Company as well as the Dublin Savings Bank. Henry Bewley, according to Annabella Mulvany, was a major investor in

Henry Bewley

the first transatlantic telegraph cable project. He was also the major investor in the Erin mine in Castrop (now Castrop-Rauxel). The Erin mine closed in 1983 when over 3,000 miners were employed but the pit-top tower has been preserved as an industrial monument.

The Bewley family are credited with breaking the tea monopoly by importing a shipload of tea direct from Canton to Dublin. Henry's youngest brother, Joshua, started the well-known cafe business which still flourishes in Dublin today.

Appendix VIII

Mulvany Family Tree (in part) •

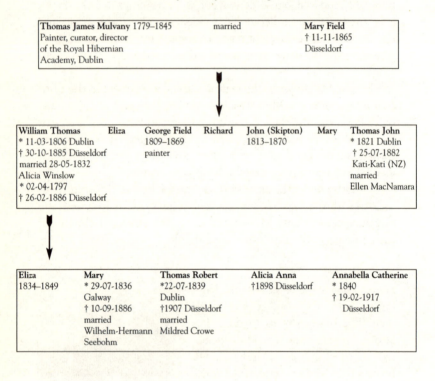

• *Official registration of births and deaths in Ireland began only around 1845, hence the missing dates.*

The Waterways of the Ruhr Today

The State Commission of which W. T. Mulvany was first chairman planned some canals of the Ruhrgebiet, which, after a century, still are a vital infrastructural component in the region's economy. Now, however, they are being refurbished to cater also for the growing leisure industry.

Picture shows Europe's major canal confluence of the Rhine-Herne Canal, the Dortmund-Ems Canal, the Wesel-Datteln Canal and the Datteln-Hamm Canal.

Bibliography

Brochure, Birr Castle Demesne.
Kurt Bloemers, *Veröffentlichungen des Archivs für Rheinisch-Westfälische Wirtschaftsgeschichte*, Band VII. Baedeker, Essen 1922.
Karl Erich Born, *Handbuch der deutschen Geschichte*. dtv, München 1975.
Asa Briggs, *The Age of Improvement 1783-1867*. Longman, London 1959.
Oskar Christ, *Chronik der Castroper Rennen 1874-1953*. Rennverein Castrop-Rauxel e.V., 1954.
Correspondence between W. T. Mulvany and his father. Published privately
Deutscher Bundestag, *Fragen an die deutsche Geschichte*. Bonn 1985.
'Glückauf', 81/84 Jahrgang, Heft 11-12, Bochum.
Erich Goerlitz, *Zeiten und Menschen*, Schöningh Verlag, Paderborn 1968.
Manfred Görtemaker, *Deutschland im 19. Jahrhundert*. Bundeszentrale für politische Bildung, Bonn 1989.
Helga Grebing, *Deutsche Geschichte der neuesten Zeit*. dtv, München 1985.
Hüttenberger, *Die Entwicklung zur Großstadt Düsseldorf*.
Robert Kane, *The Industrial Resources of Ireland*, 1845.
John Meynard Keynes, *The Economic Consequences of the Peace*. Macmillan & Co., London 1919.
Larcom, Major Thomas A., *Larcom Manuscripts*, National Library of Ireland, Dublin.
R. B. McDowell, *Social Life in Ireland 1800-45*, Cultural Relations Committee of Ireland, 1957.
Alicia A. Mulvany, *Notes on the Journey*. Published privately.
J. O'Loan, *Development of Arterial Drainage in Ireland*, Journal of the Department of Agriculture, Vol. XV, 1963.
Hermann von Pückler-Muskau, *Reisebriefe aus Irland*. Rütten & Loenig, Berlin.
Heiner Radzio, *Unternehmen mit Energie*. Econ-Verlag, Düsseldorf 1990.
Report of the Select Committee of the House of Lords into Drainage of Lands as Administered by the Board of Works, 29 June, 1852.
Rev. J. Ryan, SJ, *Studies*, Vol. XII, 1923.
Cecil Woodham Smith, *The Great Hunger*. Hamish Hamilton, London 1962.

Jochen Schmidt-Liebich, *Deutsche Geschichte in Daten*, dtv München 1981.

Dr Oskar Stillich, *Die Steinkohleindustrie*, Humboldt-Akademie, Berlin. Verlag Joh. Schnuke, Leipzig 1906.

C. M. Trevelyan, *English Social History*. Longman Green & Co., London 1942.

Universität Köln, *Kölner Vorträge zur Sozial- und Wirtschaftsgeschichte*. 1970.

Josef Windschuh, *Der Verein mit dem Langen Namen*. Dux-Verlag, Berlin 1932.

Index

Albermarle, earl of 42
Anne, Queen 16
Arndt, Gustave 79

Barry, William 42
Bath, marquess of 42
Beaumont, Lord 42
Bertelsmann 90-92
Bewley, Henry 79, 107, 151, 153
Bismark, Otto Edward Leopold 77, 87, 92, 126
Bleichröder, Gerson von 77, 79
Bloemers, Kurt 11
Brassey 61
Brunell 49
Bueck, Axel 91, 107
Burgoyne, John (Fox) 22-23, 27-28, 33, 45, 115

Clarendon, earl of 42
Clive, Robert, of India 14
Cobden, Richard 51, 91
Conrad, Wilhelm 79
Corr van der Maeren, Michael 50-52, 54-55, 57-58, 70, 74, 133
Coulson, William 63, 65
Crome, Dr F. 79
Czar of Russia, Nicholas I 152

Darwin, Charles 21
Davey, Humphrey 61, 70
Derby, Lord 49
Dinever, Lord 42
Disraeli, Benjamin, earl of Beaconsfield 13
Dooge, Prof. James 48
Dreyden 63-64
Dryden, John 64

Elliott, Mrs T. 21
Engels, Friedrich 33-34
Essex, earl of 42

Faraday, Michael 61
Funcke, Wilhelm 111

Gladstone, William Ewart 91
Glanville, earl of 42
Godeffroy, Adolf 79
Goethe, Johann Wolfgang von 15
Goodbody, Marcus 35, 74, 100, 153
Graham, James 69
Grattan, Henry 16
Griffith, I. 69
Griffith, Sir Richard 22, 27-28, 37, 43-45
Grillo, Friedrich 80

Hagemeister, von 111
Hammacher, Dr Friedrich 61, 82
Haniel, Franz 52, 61, 76, 113
Haniel, Hugo 61, 82, 113
Harrowby, earl of 42
Heinzmann, Edmund 82
Hudson, George 38
Hutchinson, Viscount 42

Johnston, Mr 21
Jones, Harry D. 28

Keynes, John Maynard 84
König, Louis Christian 62-63, 94, 101
Larcom, Major Thomas A. 43, 45-46
Lassalle, Ferdinand 73
Latimer, John 24, 133
Lattimore, William 69
Laverick, George 63, 69
Louis XIV 16
Lucan, earl of 42

Magee, G. 17
Malcolmson, David 54, 57-58, 151
Malcolmson, Frederick 59, 77
Malcolmson, Joseph 54, 56-59, 77, 79, 133, 151-152
Malcolmson, William 54, 57-59, 74
Matthew, Fr Theobald 34
Mayer, G. A. 71
McDonnell, Bernard 131
McGuerin, Louisa 93

Monteagle of Brandon, Lord 42
Moore, Tom 17
Mulvany, Alicia Anna 21, 93, 112-113, 133, 154
Mulvany, Annabella Catherine 9, 11, 17, 19, 93, 100, 111, 117, 133, 153-154
Mulvany, Eliza 17, 21, 154
Mulvany, George Field 17, 154
Mulvany, Mary 17, 74, 93, 100, 133, 154
Mulvany, Richard 17, 154
Mulvany, Thomas James 17, 20-21, 24, 30, 48, 66-67, 77, 93-94, 97, 101, 135, 154
Mulvany, Thomas Robert 11, 17-19, 22, 31-32, 49, 58, 64, 66-67, 76-77, 82, 93, 98, 110, 112-113, 115, 117, 134-135, 154
Mulvany, William Thomas 11, 17-19, 22, 31-32, 49, 58, 67, 76-77, 82, 110, 112-113, 115, 134, 154

Napoleon 17, 50
Nelson, earl of 42
Nidda, Krug von 57, 60

O'Brien, Domhall Mór 95
O'Connell, Daniel 13, 17, 41
Ovens, Ludwig von 57

Pabst, F. W. 71
Parsons, William, third earl of Rosse 40-41
Peel, John 29, 35
Perrot, S. W. 74
Perry, James and William 18, 54, 56-58, 62, 74, 77, 79, 93, 100, 133, 151, 153
Pike, Ebenezer 107
Polworth, Lord 42

Pückler-Muskau, Herman Graf von 15, 156

Robinson, William Cherry 77
Roney, Patrick C. 74
Rooney, Sir Cusack 107
Russell, Lord John 36

Salisbury, Marquess of 42
Scheel, Johann von 95
Schumann, Clara and Robert 60
Seebohm, Dr Hans-Christian 102
Seebohm, John 102
Seebohm, Mary 102, 133
Seebohm, William-Hermann 74, 100, 102
Sebastiani, Fr 65
Smith, Adam 91
Soénius, Dr Ulrich 9
Stephenson, George 49-50, 61
Stewart, George Vesey 100-101

Talbot, earl of 42
Toole, James 97-98
Trevelyan, Sir Charles 23, 28, 34, 38-39, 43-45, 48
Trinkaus, Christian 107

Velsen, von 82

Watt, James 49
Wellington, Arthur Wellesley, Duke of 13, 22
Wicklow, earl of 42
Wilde, Oscar 33
Winslow, Alicia 21, 114, 154
Winslow, Lt 21
Wodehouse, Lord 42
Wood, Sir Charles 43

Yule, Capt. 21